ACHIEVE

ORDINARY PEOPLE WHO DO EXTRAORDINARY THINGS

BY
ROB SEVERSON

All rights reserved. No part of this book may be reproduced or transmitted in any form or by any means, electronic or mechanical, including photocopying, recording, or by any information storage and retrieval system, without permission from the copyright owner.

This book was printed in the United States of America.
Copyright © 2014 Rob Severson
All rights reserved

ISBN-13: 978-1499230222
ISBN-10: 1499230222

DEDICATION

This book is dedicated to the idea that all people are created equal and have different skills, talents and interests, that when used to the best of their ability, make the world a better place. The stories of people in this book are but a few of the millions of achievers who have used their gifts to serve others and make a living. A special thanks to all of them for sharing their life stories so that others may see how they too can make it in the world.

The intent of this book is to educate and inspire. With that said, there is a study guide available. Information on this opportunity can be found on www.robseverson.com

Mike,
Thanks for sharing a "corporate" life story — and thanks for your support & friendship
Rob Severson
Philippians 4:13

TABLE OF CONTENTS

THE PROCESS
The Process of Collecting Stories		1
The Questionnaire		4
Synopsis		7
Financing Education		10

THE ACHIEVERS AND THEIR STORIES
Kevin Wilt	He put the O in Cheerios	19
Percy Greenberg	The Three P's of Success	24
Donna Erickson	Overcoming Life's Obstacles	30
Donna Amos	It Was Her Destiny	37
Jeremiah Johnson	From Jail to Achievement	43
Kim Seng	From Cambodia to An American Dream	47
Grant & Kristin Baker	How Two Achievers Found Their Soulmates!	52
Rachel Jungwirth	Family Values	60
Harold Ness	From Immigrant to The Railroad	65
Rebecca Noecker	From Harvard to High School Mentor	72
Mikhal Szabo	Africa and Hope	77
Harold Christensen	Peace Corps Teacher	83
Steve Chepokas	A Hard Knock Life	88
Brenda, Brian, Debbie	Sisters in Spirit Plus One Husband	98
Candy Swanson	A Survivor: The Little Lady with a Little Stick	114
Mike Conley	Financial Services Executive At The Top!	119
Randy Quiring	Small Town Success	126
Korey Dean, SR	The Beat Goes On	131
Phil & Nikki Foster	Opposites Attract	138
Ray Noble	A Seeker of Opportunities	146
Eddie Hutchins	Happiness is His Choice: The Man Who Has Enough	151
Mike Sims	Finding Peace and Solitude . . . And Lots of Hats!	157

THE TEAM
Rob Severson	The Author's Story	163
Charlene Torkelson	Follow Your Passion	167
Rachel Anderson	Marketing Guru	171

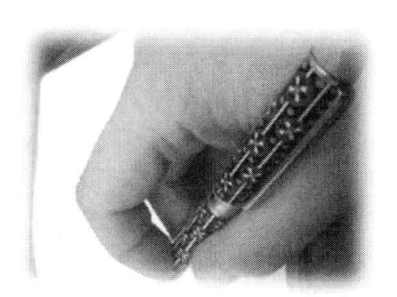

THE PROCESS

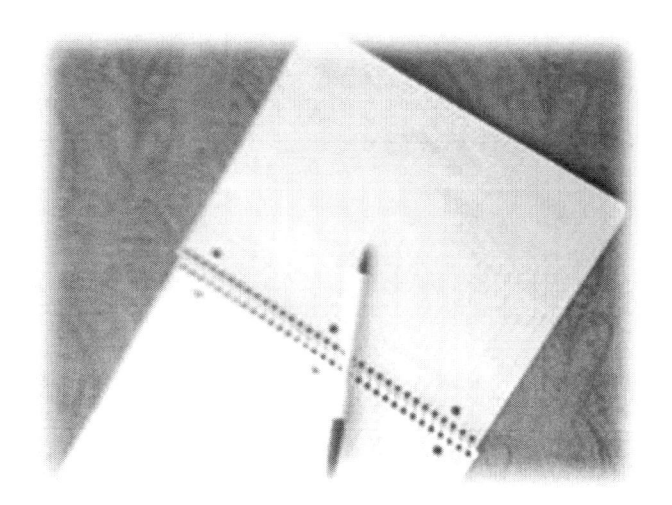

THE PROCESS OF COLLECTING STORIES

I love people and really enjoy learning about them and what they are doing with their lives. I am fortunate to know many successful people and inquisitive enough to listen to their stories. One of my most valuable assets is my contact database. I have hundreds of people I have worked with, met socially, and connected with in other ways. This database is my go-to tool that I use for my finance coaching business. I have relationships with many people who are lenders and investors that I often call on to bring financial solutions to my clients. I know what they are looking for in loans, and they respond promptly as they also know I understand finance. This tool is useful to me as I help other people with various problems. People networking for jobs who need contacts are high on my help list. In short, if I can't solve a problem, my list contains many who can. When I developed the idea for this book, I knew lots of caring people I could call who would be interested in helping others succeed and would be willing to show them through their own path to success.

There is nothing scientific about how I collected stories – no random sample, just contacting people I know who have led interesting lives or are in the process of transitioning in life. I chose to gather stories about the people we meet every day rather than the rich and famous who are well documented in other ways.

These are "ordinary" people who started out like most Americans to build businesses or careers in which they were successful by their own definition. They hope their stories will inspire readers so they, too, can become achievers in life.

I sent a questionnaire to the people I thought would help. They were asked to comment on any of the issues I included. I encouraged them to be as open as they chose to be and share anything about themselves they thought pertinent to their lives. Some shared very personal things such as disappointments or marital issues. Others focused on their professional life. None of them did this to be braggadocios; they were told the goal of the book was to show other people their pathway to success giving others ideas of their own. No one claimed their path would be best for anyone else but simply that it worked for them. All of the stories are their own based on their questionnaire responses. Some chose to write their own stories, but most I (or my editor) wrote based on what they shared in their interviews. Some referred to their faith, but their story is not meant to promote any particular religious belief in any way. Others referred to values their parents taught them as they were growing up. The values are their own and simply reported by them to tell their story as they applied. The reader is encouraged to pick and choose any advice or values from the stories they find worthwhile. Hopefully everyone will find something useful in most of them. I truly admire their willingness to share their personal stories with everyone. They all gave me permission to use their names.

The following questionnaire was given to each respondent to generate ideas for their story. Each was encouraged to freely comment on any or all of the points listed but the story is their own!

THE QUESTIONAIRE

Thank you for agreeing to be interviewed for the new book I am writing. Below is a questionnaire I'd like you to think through before we talk. You may want to make some notes so I get it right! I will use your answers to write the story of how you got where you are today.

My concept for this book is to inspire young people, whether they are coming from poverty or a poor family, a middle class family or whatever, that they can make it too. My dream is that this book will be used in schools, youth organizations, transitional groups and anywhere people are interested in getting started or working their way to a better life.

1) Name, age and current hometown
   a. Can I use your name in the book?
   b. Or do you wish to be anonymous or use a made up name?
   c. I will let you review and approve either way.

2) Family background – early upbringing through today.
   a. Values
   b. Role models
   c. Values today

3) What did you want to be when you were 5-years-old?
   a. When you were in high school or college?
   b. How close did you come to making that dream a reality?
   c. Did your dream change over time?

4) Education.
   a. Did you go to college? If so, which one, when did you graduate, and what was your major?
   b. Did you do well in college?
   c. Did you find your major directly useful?

5) First job
   a. Very first job
   b. First job starting out on your own
   c. How did you get it?
   d. Did you like it?

6) Current job
    a. If retired, what did you do last?
    b. What is your job today, and how did you get there?

7) Mentors that helped along the way
    a. People?
    b. Spouse?
    c. Other?

8) Obstacles or problems you encountered
    a. Discrimination for race, sex, religion, other?
    b. Getting fired? What did you learn?
    c. Addictions, crimes, other?

9) Defining moments in your career
    a. Biggest accomplishment
    b. Promotions?
    c. Getting fired?

10) How do you define success?
    a. Money?
    b. Power?
    c. Financial security?
    d. Happy family life?
    e. Financial freedom?

11) What do you think are the keys to your success that others may benefit from?
    a. Hard work
    b. Education
    c. Supportive spouse
    d. Values
    e. Being other's centered?

12) Have you done anything to help others?
    a. Financially?
    b. Time wise, like volunteering?
    c. Mentoring?

13) Goals for the future
    a. If retired, how do you spend your time?

       b. If mid-career, what could be next?

14) Best advice for young people
       a. Advice you received and heeded.
       b. Advice from what you have learned so far.

The only qualifications I have for people to include their stories in this book are these:

- They have gainful employment or businesses
- They are self-sufficient or working to get that way soon
- They are making a contribution to society
- They are happy in their life work and the rewards that come from it - to themselves and to others
- They want to show others a path to success if they become achievers

SYNOPSIS

"They went off to seek their fortune"

Seeking their fortune is the one thing all of the people in this book have in common. The idea of seeking one's fortune has been around for a long time. I think I first heard of it in a children's book about a young man going off to find his way in the world. Generally speaking, that fortune would mean accumulation of wealth in the form of property and money.

The people in this book also went out to seek their fortunes. However, their objectives were not just money. They saw several forms of wealth that when added up met their definition of success. They set short term and long term goals to meet their big objective of being successful. As achievers, they are constantly pursuing, meeting, or building these goals for more wealth.

The common definition of wealth for these people is summarized here. It may not apply equally for all of the people in the book, but it is a consensus of what I learned by collecting their stories.

- Inner peace: Being at peace with one's self is a major part of their wealth. These people are happy; it comes along with other capital and, for most, a relationship with a higher power.

- Education: They built a wealth of education formally or informally. They have wisdom gained from school, reading, and interacting with people.

They may have met a goal of achieving a college degree or maybe even two degrees, but would agree that life is a continuing quest to learn to build and maintain this wealth. This is essential to their ability to deal with life and its changes.

- Relationships: Perhaps the biggest component of peace, they work to maintain healthy relationships with all the people in their lives. This includes forgiving and asking for forgiveness, and focusing on others instead of themselves. They have gained their relationships through helping people and also found help from others when they needed it. Here is an interesting quote I found on relationships: "People who uplift you are the best kind of people. You don't simply keep them. You have to treasure them." — Dodinsky, an author and poet. The people in this book understand and practice both sides of that; they give and receive encouragement to/from others.

- Financial capital: Understanding the need for cash in our society, they have found honest means of procuring it to support themselves and their families. Their simple goal was to be as independent as possible by earning enough to pay their own way and support themselves. Some earned greater wealth than others, but all are meeting the goal of being capable of taking care of their needs. Most of them enjoyed the ability to give to others as well. They expressed gratitude for what they have and don't waste time envying others who have more. I think all would agree that money doesn't buy inner peace, but managing it properly does. Spending less than they earn is one of their primary goals.

- Purpose: Somewhere along their way, these people became passionate about a purpose. Usually it was to solve a problem in the world, whether by developing a product, helping other people via non-profit work, or just serving their customers' needs as best they could. And, they included employers and co-workers in their definition of customers. As they "came out of their self-interest," they gained peace and success.

All of the stories will deal with how these people are "seeking their fortune" and how they are progressing in that quest. Personally, I learned much from each one and was constantly amazed listening to their stories, their problems, and how they found opportunities to succeed. I believe there is something in this book for all readers who are seeking success.

FINANCING AN EDUCATION

We all begin our education at birth and continue with the process throughout our entire lifetime. It starts with responding, walking, talking, and progresses from there. We are like sponges absorbing all that is around us. Education is a part of our everyday life. The more we learn, the better we are able to handle any situation whether in a career, in our relationships, or with ourselves. Education makes us more confident and more competent. As we go through formal education in school, we begin to want more and more training and information. Sometimes it can be frustrating or stressful, but continuous effort brings amazing results.

Many students begin to think about their future when they reach their junior or senior years in high school. College? Trade school? Career? This becomes a life point when they start to set plans and goals for their further education. Unfortunately in this day and age, college can be expensive. Yes, there are loans available but with a little early planning, a student's debt for that education can be minimized substantially. Some parents or grandparents have the great forethought to begin a college fund when their new baby is born. However, that may not be the case for a majority of those with a wish to further their education. Students and parents should begin to look into the finances for college when in about the freshman or sophomore year of high school. There are many options that are overlooked but should be considered.

In addition to college loans, there are scholarships and grants available. Although many believe these are only options for the top academic students, this is not the case. There are scholarships presented for a variety of reasons – academic success is only one of these. Do you have special talents or skills? Music, theater, sports, community service? Do you write great essays or create wonderful art pieces? These talents may all be rewarded with scholarships or grants for college or trade school. Many organizations offer scholarships to children of their membership. It does matter who your parents are! Lions and Rotary clubs, churches, fraternal organizations, women's groups, fire fighters, music unions, etc. – all provide scholarships to their membership. Even certain cultures and nationalities provide scholarships. Norwegian societies provide scholarships if you are of Norwegian descent, and so forth. (I'm from Minnesota, so the Norwegian in me just came out!) Many businesses offer scholarships to their employees' children. There is even a scholarship for the best Duct Tape prom dress! Finding money for school may just take looking outside of the box for where you come from, what you can do, or who you know.

There is a process in finding these scholarship opportunities. The first person to see is your high school guidance counselor. They usually keep lists of available grants and scholarships – especially those that are locally provided.

Then you may look to the colleges you are thinking about attending. They also provide scholarship lists especially those funded by their alumni or groups connected to that college. Then look on-line. www.fastweb.com is an example of one site that provides lists of scholarships for students who file a profile of their interests and goals. They try to match you with choices that fit your background and future plans. E-mail updates are sent out frequently with applications and deadline information. There are several other websites also used to consolidate scholarship opportunities. Look to some of the larger businesses for their scholarships – Target, General Mills, etc. All have offers available for furthering education goals. The newspaper is another great source. Many organizations and churches list scholarship opportunities in local blurbs for community activities.

If you are a Division I or II athlete in a sport, check for the colleges with your sport to see the availability of moneys for their athletes and teams. Remember to register with the NCAA and check all eligibility requirements including academic guidelines. Club sports such as gymnastics, ultimate Frisbee, and rugby also offer scholarships for their athletes. However, remember an athletic scholarship expects performance in that sport as well as maintenance of good academic standing.

Financing an education takes a little leg work as well as effort, but it is well worth the time. Grants and loans are also available for those needing financial assistance. In order to qualify, a family must file a FAFSA each year with a review of income and financial need. This is also well worth the time and effort taken. A grant is money that is not paid back; a loan is repaid with a reasonable interest rate. When you take advantage of these loans, consider what is needed to pay them back upon graduation. Many students accumulate an unreasonable amount of debt after graduation. Take a careful look at the numbers before committing to something that may be uncomfortable later on. Many colleges also offer work-study programs – jobs through the school while a student. These are not only a great financial help but often an excellent work experience. The problem for some students with work-study programs is often you never really see (or feel!) the money as it goes directly toward your tuition costs.

Remember private colleges may appear more expensive on paper when comparing tuitions, but they also may offer a better financial package than the state schools with more grants and scholarship opportunities through their endowment funds. Private colleges also usually include room and board in their price tag. Living expenses can be more overwhelming than first anticipated. Look into what options are available for housing and meals when considering the total dollar amount spent on your education. Living at home, while not as desirable for many, may be more reasonable financially. Consider all your options when looking at the big picture. Do your homework to figure out what is really the best deal for you. Remember however, a great financial deal in a field you are not really suited for or at a college you don't really want to attend is no deal at all. It is no surprise so many students transfer to other institutions once they begin college because it wasn't at all what they expected. Take time to consider all of your options and all of your personal wants and needs for a great education and ideal career future.

THE ACHIEVERS

AND . . .

THEIR STORIES

KEVIN WILT

HE PUT THE HOLES IN CHEERIOS!

When people ask Kevin Wilt what he did at General Mills, he replies, "I put the holes in Cheerios!" Obviously he doesn't take himself too seriously! Although he ended his career with General Mills near the top as Director of Operations, he began at the bottom.

Raised in a farm family rich in values but not so rich in money, he couldn't afford to go to college. He learned a trade as a carpenter working with builders beginning in the seventh grade. By nineteen he was on his own accepting carpentry as his future. While remodeling a basement for a General Mills Plant Manager, he obviously made quite an impression. The manager asked Kevin if he would be willing to work for a big corporation — or at least try it for a year to see how he liked it. Wilt considered the benefits and the stability of GMI and decided to give it a try.

He tried General Mills for that year and stayed on. When he got married and started a family, financial reality set in! He needed to make more money and the best way would be to work his way up at GMI. To do that, he knew he had to get a college degree. So Wilt did it the hard way. GMI paid his tuition, but it took eight long years and many hours to get the degree he needed. Wilt credits his supportive wife, Debbie, who left her teaching job to stay home, raise the children, and manage the household so he could work fulltime and study. It was difficult but worthwhile. Of course values he learned as a child helped make the process easier.

During his career he was known as a problem solver — one who was never afraid to jump into a tough situation. He turned around a manufacturing facility, even though many in General Mills never thought it could be done. Always a man to freely give praise, Kevin Wilt credits that success to the team he assembled with building operational excellence into the troubled facility. With that successful operation completed, he faced more challenges as well as promotions with GMI. He was sent from his position in Ohio into a management post in the Minneapolis home office.

The move up the corporate ladder wasn't always easy. At the peak of his career, he anticipated a very large promotion that fell through. Kevin was justifiably disappointed and even considered leaving the company. After careful consideration, he decided he liked what he was doing and would continue rather than let his ego be his guide. It was a tough decision for the Wilt family, but they survived this disappointment nicely. When he retired at age fifty-five from General Mills, he was Director of Operations for the cereal division.

Kevin Wilt defines success as being at peace, having a happy family, leaving a legacy, and finding financial freedom. Always valuing others, he found mentors along the way in family, coaches, pastors, and work associates. He credits many of his personal values to his father and his favorite president, Abraham Lincoln. At the top of his value list he appreciates honesty, the Golden Rule, hard work and setting an example for others. He also sees God as impacting his life with many blessings as he did the work he needed to do. He and his wife, Debbie, have served Him in their churches as elders and deacons. That legacy lives on with his adult children who are now active in their churches as well.

As a person who centers his philosophy on others, Kevin Wilt shares these values as key to great leadership skills:

*Be a role model through ethics, integrity, and hard work

*As a leader, stretching goals creates outstanding performance, drive, opportunities, and a rallying point for a team mentality

*Create a sense of urgency and purpose

*Empowering your team and yourself avoids victims

*Hold yourself and others accountable

*Assume positive intent in others

*Give the credit to others

*The end result: Everybody wins!

At the age of fifty-three, Kevin Wilt had a heart attack. He did what was needed to improve his health dropping weight, maintaining a low salt diet, and increasing his exercise. Now at fifty-seven, he spends time with his family, golfs with wife Debbie and friends, enjoys his lake cabin, loves his home handyman projects, and travels. He is very much at peace and happily lives life. He lives his life in retirement as he did throughout his career as a role model, mentor and advisor.

AUTHOR'S COMMENTS

I met Kevin and Debbie on the golf course shortly after they joined the club. People's behavior on the golf course often reflects their total behavior. Kevin and Debbie were fun to play with, taking the game seriously but not themselves. That may sound trite, but many golfers throw tantrums, cuss and swear, and are not enjoyable to be with. Not Kevin and Debbie! I was happy to have met them. I am more pleased that I have gotten to know them better and continue to see them often at the club.

Upon learning I was writing this book, several people confirmed that Kevin had a great story and should definitely be included. Kevin caught on to my goal right away and was one of the first I interviewed for a story. He is a very humble man and didn't want to brag at all; he was hopeful that someone would learn something from how he made it.

I am most impressed with Kevin's people skills and the leadership principles he shares. I have also witnessed his skills when he was president of our golf club.

I noted in his story, as well as witnessed it at the club, that his life changed after his heart attack. He lost some weight, retired to alleviate stress, and now focuses on his health and family. His advice for weight management is this: "If it tastes good, spit it out!" He also works on his golf game by taking lessons and practicing but still is a great example for all as he takes the game seriously but not himself!

He and Debbie brighten up the golf course for all.

PERCY GREENBERG

The Three P's of Success

As Percy Greenberg walked across the tarmac for his flight, it was a very different walk than the one he took so many years ago. As a young man in Winnipeg, Canada, he walked out of school in the ninth grade. His early life was not easy — far from it. He grew up in an atmosphere that was abusive both physically and verbally. Often times he was on the giving end of the abuse. Our school system today would consider a boy like Greenberg to be a "troublemaker" or bully. But Greenberg was determined to prove those who thought he wouldn't amount to anything wrong. Very wrong! In hindsight, his lack of formal education has become one of Greenberg's greatest regrets. He has never been proud of his decision to leave school.

Coming from a trucking family, he found work as a cross-country truck driver. The work was hard and physically tiring, but it fostered one of his lifelong loves. Trucks! He discovered he loved to drive trucks — the big ones — the ones that drive cross-country. Today if asked to list his greatest talents he includes 1) driving trucks 2) working with metal and 3) flying. True to form, Greenberg made all three central to his successes in life. He and his brother own a trucking company together with those same big rigs he drove as a young man.

Married to his wife Bernice for over fifty years, Greenberg has two children and four grandchildren. Early on in his marriage, he moved to the United States for the opportunity to better support his growing family by working in a smelting company. Although raised a Canadian, his American citizenship has become a great source of pride. "I am a citizen by choice, not by an accident of birth," he explained.

As he worked his way up in the metal company, he and his partner Norman Goldetsky decided to start their own company, Copper Sales, building it into one of the top architectural metal manufacturing companies in the United States with five locations and over five hundred employees. The company provided not only financial opportunity but also a creative outlet. During his years at Copper Sales, Greenberg invented several key machines used to revolutionize the metal industry. He currently holds about forty inventions (the exact number is hard for him to remember) for concepts and equipment he developed. Even today next to his office desk he has hung a white board allowing him to draw and illustrate the concepts he creates and ponders. The ideas flow constantly with lines and arrows showing how something might — or might not — work. In 2005 a multibillion dollar corporation discovered Greenberg's company and recognizing the quality of his vision purchased Copper Sales as their flagship metal manufacturing company.

Another success story for Greenberg has been his airplane. This may be the one he is most proud to share. In this story, he relates one of his biggest fears — flying. Copper Sales required he travel around the country for meetings. However, he was afraid to fly. When driving to a meeting became impossible at one point, he decided to face his fear head on. Not only was he determined to get up into an airplane, but he decided to go even further. He learned how to fly himself, got his pilot's license, and bought his own plane. Now that is the way to deal with fear!

Now over seventy years old, Percy Greenberg continues to maintain his businesses and his office. Punctually each morning at 7:30 he arrives at the office. His schedule remains the same. First, coffee — strong — then down to business. His business ventures these days vary. He invests in others and their dreams providing venture capital to those in need of extra funds just like those who provided funds to him as he began to build his own businesses. Greenberg believes in listening to other people and allowing others to fulfill their plans. He advises others to "surround yourself with people who know what you don't". And he does just that. He connects with other people and their ideas giving each one careful thought and opinion.

Percy Greenberg has always believed success comes from three principles: passion, pride, and perception. He explains "pride" is not only in your work but also in your surroundings. "I had the cleanest metal factory anywhere!" he declares with pride. That is what made the business a success. Passion might be self-explanatory, but "perception," the one element most difficult to define, is what Greenberg calls "eye catching". He continues, "Perception brings positive attention." He has always looked for these same values in the people he surrounded himself with in his companies and partnerships. Pride, passion, and perception.

Acquaintances describe Percy Greenberg as "very generous and intelligent". Intelligence is quite a compliment for someone who left school in the ninth grade. Although he has never recommended anyone take school lightly and has always counted his lack of formal education as his biggest regret, Greenberg sees life itself as an education. He learned his life lessons well and stands out as a role model for pride, passion, perception, generosity, and yes . . . education. We are all offered a lifelong experience to educate ourselves. If we learn from life's opportunities as Percy Greenberg did, we will find an exciting journey filled with a wealth of knowledge.

AUTHOR'S COMMENTS

I was president of the firm who financed Percy's business and acted as an advisor to him early in my finance coaching career. The man amazed me from our first meeting!

He often laments the fact that he never had an education, but this man can figure things out as well as anyone I have ever met. He can meet with bankers and others wearing a suit and tie then put on coveralls, go out to the plant, and fix machines. He never studied sales, but he has about forty inventions for products he designed to make his industry better. He did this by understanding needs, problems, and then providing solutions. That is a true salesman - find the need and sell the solution!

I really admire Percy's ability to listen to other people who know something he doesn't. I was an expert in bank financing, and he once told me, "Severson, even if we aren't successful in getting financed, I learned a lot about banking from you!" I am sure he learned from other people given his humility and desire to learn what he needed to be successful. As a "self-made man," he quickly figured out he needed good people surrounding him to be successful.

I learned another thing about Percy – his loyalty to people who help him. I can attest to it as Percy was very loyal to me. He was always grateful for the financing he received when I was president of the company aiding him when his company fell victim to an internal fraud. The first project I did as an advisor was a little difficult, but we got it done. My compensation was very fair. I helped him with additional financing over time that was not so difficult. He compensated me very generously as he was doing substantially better. He may not have even needed me at some point, but he knew I could help and was loyal to me for being there when he previously really needed my support.

I continue to visit him on occasion just to catch up and see what he is doing. He is one man who won't retire and just play golf. His big enjoyment is helping other people with their companies via investing and mentoring. He has helped a lot of people get started and grow their businesses successfully.

When I asked him to share his story for this book, he was a little reluctant given his humility. But when I explained that his story could inspire some young person to achieve something worthwhile in their lives, he was all in. He commented that he wished he was ten years younger as he sees opportunity everywhere. Where others see problems, he sees opportunity!

DONNA ERICKSON

OVERCOMING LIFE'S OBSTACLES

Donna Erickson began life already facing a series of obstacles. Born into an Iowa farm family with six brothers, she vividly recalls the obstacles a girl — or woman — faced in the 1950's. Only thirty-eight years before her birth in 1913, women received their rights, but change was slow in coming. Women's opportunities were just beginning to shift with classic television shows like "Father Knows Best," "Leave it to Beaver," "Ozzie and Harriet," and "The Donna Reed Show" continuing to suggest women not work outside the home. Donna faced a life of experiencing the place a woman held in society. She began to realize the important thing was to recognize those obstacles and either work around them, or better yet, eliminate them all together. She understood from an early age that education was the key factor to bypass the more established female careers of nursing, teaching, and above all else, being a secretary. Regardless of what your own obstacles might be, Donna explains, "Success is only how one interprets life in the end."

Erickson found a huge shift in women's rights occurred in 1979 when the Convention of All Forms of Discrimination Against Women was adopted by the United Nations. Historically, this was an important event for women universally.

"However," she continues to explain, "the 'psychology of mind' that should go along with such a shift doesn't necessarily happen just because a bill is passed or an amendment made. Prejudice is an ugly obstacle that has stood in the way of many talented people keeping them stuck in stereotypical careers."

In addition to the obstacles she faced as a woman, Donna Erickson also began her life in poverty. Her family was poor. Her father didn't own the family farm; he rented from someone the family knew as the "Landlord". Over half of the annual profit from the crops would go to that "Landlord". After deducting the cost of the seed, planting, and harvesting, there was little profit for the farmer who rented land. Early on, Donna was determined not to work for anyone else unless absolutely necessary. The "Landlord" obstacle became a motivational factor for Donna to discover ways to work for herself. Of course she had lots of jobs to provide money along the way, but she knew "having a boss" would someday have to disappear in order for her to be truly happy.

Foregoing college immediately after high school, she ran off to marry an Air Force officer. Lesson one: Sometimes you have to relocate in order to get past the obstacles standing in the way of your happiness or success. Be willing to relocate! Lesson two: Make sure you know what kind of environment you are moving into and know what kind of people will be in that environment! She learned that cultivating "discernment" is a very important factor in making important personal and professional decisions. "Rule of thumb, obstacles will always get in the way. whether fabricated or real. If you get passed one, there will always be another big one you run right smack into! Be prepared for that and don't let it bring you down! Don't let it stop you from doing what you know you should be doing with your life. Keep your dreams in your heart, don't let them disappear, wait for the right time to make them real."

Donna discovered her new obstacle was education. During the next twelve years, she was married and divorced twice with three small daughters. Without an education, she recognized she had little hope of providing for herself and her children — or ever doing what she truly wanted to do in life. Although the thought of going to college was pushed to the back of her mind, she realized without it, she felt a deep rooted kind of incongruence in her life. Lesson learned: pay attention to what your heart tells you and when something reappears over and over again, you need to do something about it. She began to consider an important element in her life — TIME! She was thirty-two years old with no education. As she thought about the next eight years, she began to ask several important questions. Did she want to turn forty with or without a degree? There was no getting over the reality that she would certainly turn forty. The time between thirty-two and forty could be used in many different ways. How would she use this chunk of time? The answer to these questions always came up the same. She needed to get a BA, and she had eight years to do it. Next question, was this feasible? She determined it was. The first goal was to get an Associate

Degree because at least with this degree she would be happier and with better opportunities. It was a start! Borrowing money from a friend, she began to take classes. Within the next five years, she not only received her Associate Degree but also a BA in Human Services. Although it was not traditional by most standards, it was a BA degree. With this she was able to look for different options, consider different kinds of jobs, and make more money.

Now she began to ponder an interesting new question. What did she really want to do if she could have any career at all? The answer was to have her own counseling practice. For that, however, she needed a Master's Degree in Counseling/Psychology. Donna searched and found a program that allowed her to attend the first semester of school under a probation period to see if she could do the work. If not, she would be out. If she could, she would continue like all of the others in the program. Because she had completed a not so traditional BA degree, she was not prepared for the graduate level classes. She continued to work to provide for her family, and her children needed her time and attention. With all of these obstacles, she recalls this to be a life changing experience. She knew she had this one chance to make it work. And make it work she did! At the end of the semester, she stared at her grades — all A's. Lesson learned: if you really want to accomplish something, there are very few obstacles that will get in your way.

She graduated with her Masters in Counseling/Psychology just as she had planned and went to work for someone else. After two years in the field of crisis intervention, she had to face the biggest decision she ever had to make. Did she continue to give half of what she made to the "Landlord" or did she start her own business? The "Landlord" was really safe, but also limiting. There was only one thing to do — in 1994 she left the safe job and incorporated her own counseling practice. Lesson learned: no one but you can make your dreams come true.

There were times along the way toward Donna's dream when she looked at all the obstacles. Lesson learned: They are just obstacles and nothing more. Sometimes you have to work with the obstacles, sometimes you have to go around the obstacles, but if possible, just eliminate them. You don't want them to come back even bigger and more powerful later on in life. The most important lesson learned? There will be people who will come into your life who want to help you become successful. Donna Erickson feels blessed to say she let those who truly cared help move with her toward her life goals. Teachers, pastors, and friends all encouraged her and kept her motivated during the really difficult times. The strongest motivation of all? Her faith! It was truly the only thing she could always depend on to be there for her all of the time. Without her faith, Donna doesn't believe she could have done all she had to do — one day at a time! Lesson learned: follow your heart, keep your faith, and don't give up. It took her forty-two years before she could do what she really wanted to do. Now she has another twenty to enjoy it all. And it was all worth it. Donna's final piece of advice is, "Never give up your dreams!"

AUTHOR'S COMMENTS

When I have a problem, I usually go first to my contact base which is loaded with people in various industries. But when I had a problem with alcohol, I went to the internet as I wanted to keep my problem under wraps for a while. That is where I discovered Donna. I was interested in finding a Christian counselor because of my faith. Donna fit the bill.

It took a few sessions of talking for me to build trust in this stranger. She was a patient listener, so it became easier over time. She was always non-judgmental, and I came to understand I could tell her anything. Her subsequent advice was very worthwhile too. She recommended I go to Hazelden, a treatment center, for additional help. I spent three weeks at Hazelden but believe the time I spent with Donna was my best treatment.

Since her therapy was "all about me," I didn't know much about Donna until we became friends months after our sessions. Then one day Donna shared her story with me. I had realized earlier she had been divorced and had a great new marriage, but that was about it. When she told me the rest, it got really interesting. Actually, we had some great laughs and giggles as she was telling me about the crazy things she had done throughout her life. I'm always impressed with people who can look back on their mistakes and see the humor involved.

She is in a business where she helps people overcome their problems with a focus on those with drug and alcohol issues. In the early days of treatment programs, they used to hire addicts and alcoholics who could relate with the patients. Donna didn't have addiction problems, but she certainly knew how to relate to people with the problem. She was an overcomer herself! Now that I know her story, I am even more impressed with her friendly smile and positive attitude; she is even more inspiring to me.

I truly admire her for having the courage and stamina to get her education and fulfill her dream of helping other people. She did a great job telling her story and giving valuable advice to everyone. She has learned much through experience as well as through education. I'd recommend her to anyone with alcohol or drug problems.

DONNA AMOS

IT WAS HER DESTINY

Donna Amos always knew she wanted to be a business owner but didn't realize it was her destiny! After high school, Donna went to college for two years to study business administration, got married, and began a new job. Already using her networking skills, she took a job in an Ohio public defender's office, but she soon made a headlong leap into business with two friends. The venture was a support service for small businesses. She kept her day job as she developed the service business on weekends and evenings. Within eighteen months, the enterprise had failed miserably, the partners ended up in court fighting over the minor issues, and the friendships were lost in the process. In hindsight, she realized she learned more from the failure than she would have from a success. She learned she liked being in charge and making the decisions necessary for a successful endeavor.

At age twenty-six, she and her husband started a family, and she made a decision to stay at home with her sons during their early years. Taking a practical approach, Donna started a daycare in her home while developing a consulting business. Her consulting business helped individuals develop a budget (and stay on it) to gain control over their money issues and get out of debt. She found there was a need for her service in small businesses as well. She began to identify the reasons small business owners were struggling financially. Common problems for most were inconsistent marketing and flow of prospects into the pipeline. So she began to shift her focus toward developing the market piece for the small business person and following up mailings with telemarketing calls. Donna soon had a team of six working out of their own homes making those calls.

In 1994, with her sons in school full time, Donna sought opportunities away from home. She began to work for a nationally known real estate company. With a promotion to management in 1997, she sensed something was amiss with those she worked with in the real estate profession. She believed they needed to view their jobs as if they owned their own businesses. Through her growing network, she stumbled onto Thomas Leonard, often referred to as the "father of coaching," and immediately knew she was missing that skill. She cleverly bartered her services as a website builder with the International Coach Academy School in exchange for training in their coaching program. That educational opportunity made everything come together.

During the next ten years in the real estate business, she recruited, trained, and coached agents to believe in and treat their jobs as if the business was their own. During the last seven years of her management career, she also built and maintained a steady flow of private coaching clients. Throughout those management years, however, she still felt the bite of that entrepreneurial bug. She wanted her own business! Donna decided to take her business coaching skills to the next level but needed to quit her high paying job to do so. She explains, "You know the fear of stepping out keeps us stuck. What we believe is security is really more like a straight jacket keeping us prisoner. I decided to break out of the prison. Although I enjoyed the work I was doing, there was still something missing." And that missing piece was she wasn't pursuing the passion to be on her own.

Donna had some college education and supplemented that by taking the coaches' training program. An avid reader, she also read and studied all the business success books she could find, absorbing that information for use in her coaching business. She had a passion to be the best coach she could be for her clients. A consummate networker, her contacts recognized her skills and sent clients her way. She became a trainer for business support groups, produced free webinars, and used social media to reach out to people. All of these brought even more relationships and business opportunities.

Amos attributes her success to her strong desire to help businesses create and maintain profitable practices. She has an innate ability to define problems and create solutions to keep businesses moving forward. She continues to read books to help her deal successfully with her clients. With her "antenna" up constantly looking for new networking and business opportunities, she values relationships above all else. She continues to discover other business needs and creates marketable solutions for these issues. In her words she "asks for the order!" — an attribute sometimes neglected by those not involved with sales!

She says, "Today I love what I do. Although it was scary to give up a very lucrative paycheck, it has been so worth the change. I dance and sing on my way to the shower. Once in the shower I meditate, repeat my affirmations, and focus on my plans for the day. When I step out I feel excited and empowered."

She certainly is a natural coach!

AUTHOR'S COMMENTS

The current trend is to use social media for selling product, building relationships, and learning about happenings in one's field. I joined LinkedIn and Facebook with those goals in mind – especially the goal of generating sales for my first book.

Somewhere in the process of building contacts, I connected with Donna Amos. I can't remember how we found each other, but I soon discovered she is very creative. A couple of years ago she offered a free half hour of consulting to anyone who wanted to talk. I took her up on that offer, and soon we had set a date for a phone conversation.

What I remember the most about that phone call were the laughs we had. She was delightful with a great sense of humor. Interspersed in our laughter, she also gave me several great tips for marketing my book. Most of the offers for free consulting turn out to be a sales pitch with little value to the caller. I expected to get a hard pitch from Donna but it never came. She did offer her services, but I sensed her intention really was to give some of her time to others. Shortly after, she referred me for a podcast interview with someone she had met on LinkedIn. It was great exposure for me.

To thank her for the time, I sent her a copy of my first book. The old saying in the book business is that nobody reads free books, but she actually read it. Moreover, she did a book review for me and encouraged me to continue my marketing efforts as she saw the value of my book. Of course that made me feel good, but by that time I recognized she was just honestly encouraging me. I haven't had a need for her services yet, but if I did, I would quickly turn to someone who is sincerely interested in my success. She demonstrated that – the best sales pitch of all!

Her story of building her business is a testament to her service nature. She has earnestly set out to learn what problems small businesses have and then provide services for the solutions. Additionally she sends out encouragement emails frequently with quotes from great people. I can tell that her consulting service is loaded with encouragement!

When I called her for the interview, we once again got into a laughing spree. I very much enjoy dealing with people with a sense of humor. But the important thing to learn from Donna's story is her ability to fully engage in a service/consulting business with the first goal to provide value to her clients – for her, the second to make a living.

JEREMIAH JOHNSON

FROM JAIL TO ACHIEVEMENT

Sitting in a jail for six months gives a person time to ponder about lots of things. That is how Jeremiah Johnson concluded he was on the wrong life path. He was in jail for a drunk driving sentence and had been using drugs for most of his adult life, including alcohol, marijuana, acid, cocaine, and other party drugs. He started to realize that his lifestyle could only result in either jail for a longer length of time or possible death. That was the point he decided he didn't want either; he wanted to do something more with his life.

Growing up on a small farm, Jeremiah learned something about physical work and taking care of the things you need to survive like feeding and caring for the animals that become food, chopping wood for heat, and other tasks that made it possible to live. His family had a decent home, but he didn't fully appreciate it until his parents divorced, forcing him and his mom to move to a much smaller home. They lived close to poverty level until his mother moved on to get an education and a good job.

Jeremiah did know how to work and made a little money working for landscapers and snow plow operators. He was inquisitive enough to actually learn the businesses that would help him later on when he got his life straightened out.

He had developed a skill set that would eventually allow him to earn his own way in the world.

As many people who wander in life, he and a girlfriend moved to Missouri for a few years continuing their drinking and drugging lifestyles. He was arrested several times on disorderly conduct charges and drunk driving that resulted in short stints in jail. He wasn't going anywhere in Missouri, so he moved to Fargo to live with his father. This was where his lifestyle worsened, and he ended up with a six month jail sentence. Then he started to figure it out!

Shortly after getting out of jail, he was accepted into Teen and Adult Challenge, a Christian addiction treatment center. While in jail, he recognized that God had a plan for his life, and it wasn't for him to just get high and coast through life. He began to realize that life might be a short one given his habits. As he put it, "I had become a bystander in life and just watched life go by getting high to cope." His Teen Challenge experience gave him hope, faith, and motivation to succeed helping other people along the way.

Fortunately, he had learned a trade early on. His work with landscapers now paid off. He also knew how to take care of the tools and equipment he needed in order to be successful. He had learned that growing up with his father. So he went out on his own to start a tree trimming and landscaping business.

It wasn't easy and had few immediate rewards. He went out to his garage one day to discover his equipment had been stolen. He had purchased it piece by piece as he could afford without amassing any financial obligations to repay. It was a disappointment for him, but he picked himself up and began to increase his equipment inventory all over again. It was touch and go for quite a while, but his needs were being met along the way. That increased his faith as well.

He continued to buy expensive equipment as best he could. Things like Bobcat graders and "cherry pickers" that lift people to trim high branches were necessary for his business, and he bought them as he could without accumulating large amounts of debt. Little by little he has grown his business to one that now provides a nice living for his young family.

His first marriage combined drugs and mutual unfaithfulness which was obviously a recipe for disaster. It ended before he entered Teen Challenge. Soon after leaving Teen Challenge, he met his wife Jill, who had also been through the Teen Challenge program. Coming together with the same faith, she has become a great soul mate for him. Married, they now have a two children, with the addition of their baby girl born April 5, 2014. They are doing very well with their business and family, and more importantly to them, spiritually.

One of their proudest accomplishments is reaching a point where they can afford to give to others. They tithe 10% of their income to their church, Teen Challenge, and other missionary efforts. Jeremiah has now learned the joys of giving! At the age of 38, he has come a long way. He has turned his life around rather than continue in his former lifestyle that certainly would have ended in a young death or jail. He is now an achiever!

AUTHOR'S COMMENTS

Jeremiah looks like a woodsman! Tall, well built with reddish hair and beard, he fits the bill perfectly. I found him via my contact database as I needed to get a tree cut down. I received several bids, and Jeremiah was in the ball park so I hired him. I admit I also wanted to give work to a man who had turned his life around. Many in my neighborhood have also had him cut trees in their yards as he is very dependable, fair, and efficient.

His story is one of great life changes and becoming an achiever. I hear many stories like this but want to point out that Jeremiah and others like him are in the minority of addicts. As Jeremiah figured out, most of them do die, go to jail, or just live mediocre lives in search of the next high. Jeremiah would never want to give anyone the impression that it is easy to overcome addiction. He is one of the fortunate ones.

I have only spent a little time with him, but it is obvious to see how his faith is foremost in his life. He really does enjoy the ability to give money back to Teen Challenge and other charities he believes help people. He is a caring woodsman!

KIM SENG

FROM CAMBODIA TO AN AMERICAN DREAM

The Vietnam War left many casualties, both in America and Southeast Asia. Thousands of Americans died in an effort to keep communism from those Asian countries. The war was unpopular here, but it had an even more tragic impact on the countries fighting the battles —especially if you were on the wrong side!

Stranded in a military camp, Kim Seng had to evacuate his home and belongings to get on a ship out of his native Cambodia. The communists were taking over personal property and executing military people who opposed them. Kim was in the navy and feared he would be a target. He wanted to save his family and find new opportunity somewhere else. He wasn't sure where that would be.

Kim's position as an officer in the navy had been very rewarding. He had a chauffeur, a cook, and a sailor to do his housework. Plus it provided a good paycheck. His in-laws, with land and real estate holdings, were considered wealthy by normal standards. Their property was confiscated, and they were moved to a farm to work. Leaving behind their former lifestyle was difficult, but they had no choice. It was time to think about their future.

Kim and his wife, Naychy, were shipped to the Philippines then flown to Camp Pendleton in California to await their ultimate, unknown destination. They brought their 23 day old baby, Dalia, and Naychy's 11 year-old brother and 12 year-old sister with them. It would be a big adventure for all of them! In 1973 a sponsor came forward to bring them to Minnesota.

Kim thought he must be going to Siberia when they told him it was cold in Minnesota. He got off the plane in July dressed in a parka and wrapped in blankets. Imagine his surprise when he met his hosts dressed in shorts and tee shirts! This was his first bit of good news!

A Christian American businessman sponsored Kim and his family's move to America. The businessman and his church were largely responsible to help Kim acclimate to his new life in America and give support to him in other ways as well. But he hadn't come for handouts, he came for opportunity! Initially he needed those handouts, or "hand ups" as he called them. First, he had to improve his English proficiency to communicate with those he met. He attended college to study English and accounting hoping to get a degree that would qualify him for a better job opportunity. Eventually he would work for a large computer firm, a stockbroker, and finally an insurance agency as a specialist in communication with other Cambodians.

Kim's wife, Naychy, started a sewing business to help support the family. She also did day care in her home while Kim worked two jobs to earn enough to meet their needs. With the two working, they were able to support themselves and begin to give back to their church and the others who had helped them along the way.

But Kim wanted more for his family than just his jobs could provide. He had a strong belief in responsibility and wanted to raise his children as best he could. He wanted them to have good educations and live comfortably. More importantly, he wanted to be able to give back even more to others just as he had received when he arrived in America. So Kim and Naychy worked hard and saved all they could. They both had the same goal — to be in business for themselves.

As their savings grew, they invested in a Subway store and later a donut shop. With this new found fortune, Kim invested in some real estate and increased his financial worth upon resale. In later years, they purchased a small farm hoping someday to sell it to a land developer as their retirement option.

Kim is truly living the American dream. His biggest obstacle was learning to speak English well, and he did his best to become as proficient as possible. He credits his success to working hard, saving money for business investments, and having the courage to invest when the opportunity arose. He also credits his Christian faith for giving him the courage and confidence to take a chance with his business options. His is a true example of a great American immigrant success story! He has proven America to be the land of opportunity; if you pursue success, you will find it. Their children were fortunate to receive good educations and an American life free from the threats their parents had endured in their native Cambodia. They also have the good fortune of having strong role models to emulate! An American dream comes true.

AUTHOR'S COMMENTS

I met Kim at my church and frequently saw him as we lived in the same neighborhood a couple of doors apart. We would ride the bus to work together and chat about what we were doing and how things were going. I was always impressed by his optimism as he was getting his education and working at the same time. He clearly wanted to have a life as good, or better, than he had in Cambodia. I learned he was quite well off in Cambodia and wondered if he would succeed here as well. It was easy to tell he had goals and was working hard to achieve these.

Many people in my church were willing to help him with money, clothes, or other basic needs when he first arrived in America. He was very active in our church; he wasn't just there for the assistance. I lost track of him when he moved to another home a distance away and left our church. I often wondered what had become of Kim – had he been just a taker using our church for support? Then I spoke with someone who knew what Kim had been doing the past few years. He had become an entrepreneur! And a very successful one at that! More impressively were his efforts to help other Southeast Asians settle into the American way of life. He had left our church to join a church populated with other Southeast Asians and support them through what he had learned during his own journey. So he wasn't a taker after all; he was indeed a giver!

I very much respect what he has accomplished. He assimilated into the American culture while maintaining his Cambodian heritage via his church friendships. He came here with his wife, mother-in-law and a few children basically with no material possessions. But he saw, and still sees, America as the land of opportunity. He is a modern day example of an immigrant making the American dream come true!

GRANT AND KRISTIN BAKER
HOW TWO ACHIEVERS FOUND THEIR A SOULMATES!

People seek companionship in many places, many with the goal of finding a spouse or soul mate. They go to bars, clubs, churches, and workplaces to find someone they want to spend the rest of their lives with. Being early achievers makes things easier on the path through life. It also puts achievers together as they develop like-minded friendships and relationships. Here is a story of two young achievers who found each other on their paths to success.

Grant's story

Born into a family with strong values, Grant's parents instilled in him the necessity of honesty, hard work, faith, and selflessness. Both of his parents went to college, so it was an easy decision on his part to do the same. It was just part of that value system. He always had a job while he was in high school and learned hard work and being productive for the employer were the keys to success. Another job benefit was they paid him so he could save for college and have some fun once in a while too!

Grant started at the University of Minnesota thinking he would become an attorney but migrated to finance early in his college years. He had good grades majoring in Economics and Finance even though he didn't like some of the math courses, especially calculus! But he got through the math and came out with a 3.5 GPA prepared to get a high-powered job in the finance arena.

While attending a career fair at the University, Grant met with several recruiters he thought he would like to work with after graduation. Wells Fargo Consumer Finance was about the last one on his list, but he talked with them anyway. Consumer Finance offers good opportunities but many are not interested in this type of work. Much of it is spent on the phone selling small loans to consumers or refinancing money problems. It can be hard work, but those who can do it do very well. At the career fair, the Wells Fargo Financial was the best option for his needs at the time, so he took it. Other opportunities may have been more lucrative but were based mostly on commissions, and he needed immediate income. His goal was to get his school loans paid and some savings in the bank so he would have a sound financial foundation to start his post-college life. Rather than spend several months looking for what might be his dream job, he was eager to get started paying off his college debt. At the time it was a tough job market, so he took the best opportunity to begin his career. He realized he did not know what his dream job was as he had never had what he considered a "real job". He saw this new opportunity as the foundation of a career!

Success came to Grant early on in the consumer finance business. He became one of the top performers in his office and was rewarded with several promotions and pay increases. Maybe more importantly, he learned a lot about personal finance from his customers. As he would say, "I learned what not to do!" He talked with and financed many people with deep financial problems, large amounts of debt, and seemingly no way out. Most of them reached that point by spending more than they earned, and he counseled them to get their finances in order. It also cemented his decision to live at home to build some savings and get his college loans paid off quickly. Not many college graduates want to live with mom and dad, but it gave him a chance to get solvent which was his immediate goal. He gained confidence in the frugal mentality in which he was raised and did not want to have the problems he saw in with customers!

In addition to being a star performer at work, he continued networking to find better opportunities for his skills. He had built a good foundation in his first career and was ready to move on, hopefully to some of the companies higher up on his list than consumer finance had been.

Kristin also worked for Wells Fargo Financial as a sales manager. That is how they met!

Kristin's story

At the same time Gant was growing up in the city, Kristin was growing up in North Dakota. That may seem like worlds apart, but values are not relegated to locality or the size of a town. Kristin's parents taught her many of the same things as Grant's parents taught him. She learned the values of love, selflessness, kindness, gratitude and faith to name a few. Her role models were grandparents and other family members. Her father passed away when she was thirteen, so she experienced life with a single parent. It is always traumatic for a young person to lose a parent, but it brought her a stronger faith and a better understanding of life.

Kristin started college with the goal of becoming a teacher and went so far as to do her student teaching. During the process she discovered her real passion was problem solving and the mental stimulation that comes with that process. She did not dislike teaching and may return to that goal someday. She graduated with degrees in Honors and English and was set to determine how this would fit into her future plans.

Her mother recommended she become a lawyer because of her academic excellence but that was not her interest. She applied to graduate school hoping to pursue a degree in writing but was not accepted. So she focused in on her interest to help other people solve their problems. Almost by accident she fell into a job at Wells Fargo Financial. She had been working as a waitress when a friend suggested she should try banking. She soon discovered she liked solving people's financial problems and listening to their stories. She had been a bit shy growing up and found it a great experience to come out of her shell and talk with so many people. She also realized her teaching interest could be used as she counseled people on their financial situations. It may be strange for an English major to go into consumer finance, but Kristin admits it served her well. She found communication was tantamount to a business career as well as the critical thinking skills that accompany it. She became so proficient in her work that she was promoted to a branch sales manager. Then she met Grant!

Grant and Kristin together

Because they were in the same business and at the same company, these two already had common interests in the consumer finance business. Both liked the idea of helping other people with their financial problems by either counseling or lending them money to reorganize their debts. Both of them were frugal and had goals of improving their lives. They also discovered they had the same values and upbringing so it was a natural match. In addition, they shared a faith, a desire to succeed, an understanding of the importance of giving to others, and a mutual goal to accomplish these things. Grant eventually took a new job in the health care business, and Kristin was offered a different position at Wells Fargo. Each had been successful in their first jobs, and this allowed them to move on to bigger and better opportunities.

They were married a few years ago and now have a baby daughter they adore. This changed their lives as they began to recognize differences in their priorities. Grant travels frequently, and Kristin supports this by assuming a single parenting role during the week. Kristin took a position in the mortgage banking department – a position with less travel but great earning potential. They bought a home and have a mortgage that is easily manageable. The plan was to support the mortgage payment with only one of their incomes so they did not depend on both of them working. They have a good plan in place!

Unlike many young people, these achievers set financial goals for themselves and are meeting these. Their shared financial goal is to earn money to support themselves and to give to others. They believe it is good to honestly and ethically earn enough money without sacrificing time with family and friends. They understand the necessity of helping those in need as well as supporting their church and other charities. They already give generously from their income to their church and various charities. The goals they have to earn money are not greedy but rather generous! They may never have what people refer to as a "dream job," but instead have set their mutual goal to have a "dream life"!

Although young – Grant is only twenty-eight and Kristin is thirty – they have already come a long way. They have reached their successes by setting and meeting goals and living by the value system they were taught as children. They may have some challenges along the way, but their values will get them through any obstacles. With common values and goals, their marriage will certainly endure. They are soul mates in every way!

Now they are focused on raising their daughter with the same values they have and helping others as much as they can. They both approach their careers as being others-centered, and that is what allows their achievements today. What they need now is to keep on doing what they have been doing. It seems to be a formula for success.

AUTHOR'S COMMENTS

I first met Grant about twenty-five years ago when his family moved in next door to mine. As a young child, he was a scrawny kid with lots of energy and that energy has never left him! We have become close friends with his parents and all three children. It has been a pleasure to have them as neighbors. It is also fun to hear stories about the pranks the siblings play on each other now as well as when they were younger. They are a very closely knit family.

All three of the Baker children learned to work at a young age always taking on a variety of summer jobs. This prepared them for their future work when adults – Grant in health care consulting, Jared in the ministry, and Greta in marketing. I don't think they were in any way surprised by the real world work environment!

I used to hire the Baker boys to mow my lawn and shovel the driveway. Their father is a perfectionist, so I knew they were well trained for these tasks! They were very dependable, and I missed them when they moved on to college and their future endeavors.

As Grant matured, we would talk frequently. He never talked about loving money, but it was clear he wanted financial success. The old term "compassionate conservatives" would certainly apply to Grant and Kristin. They invest and spend very carefully. The only foolish investment I ever heard Grant make was when he bought a Green Bay Packer debenture. The only value for that investment is to frame and hang it on the wall. But that is excusable for a rabid Packer fan!

Many people don't understand those who have lofty financial goals. It is assumed they are greedy and self-absorbed. I watched Grant grow up and never thought of him in those terms even for a moment. When I wrote Grant and Kristin's story from their responses to my questionnaire, it became evident they were definitely others-centered people. Each approaches their job with a servant's mentality toward both their customers and their employers. They seek opportunities for advancement with the understanding it is what they produce for the business that merits promotion. My experience tells me not all people think that way; many are just in it for themselves.

Most impressive is that they generously give to their church and other charities. Grant didn't mention he supports his brother who is an overseas pastor/missionary. He didn't have to tell me; I figured it out myself!

Now it is fun to see them visit with their young daughter, Audra. They are clearly living a life of joy, and I look forward to enjoying this family for years to come!

RACHEL JUNGWIRTH

FAMILY VALUES

Every family has values. Some that are instilled in their children serve them well. Others don't. Rachel Jungwirth was fortunate as the values taught by her parents have served her well. She grew up in a smaller community in a family with an average income. Both parents worked hard to provide for their family. Her dad was in the insurance business, and her mom had a manufacturing job on an assembly line. Indeed, they were an average American family.

They may not have been rich, but they were wealthy in values! Her parents taught her to be honest, do what you say you are going to do, work hard, have faith, and get an education. Rachel's parents had not gone to college. As Rachel would say, it was not a question of whether she and her siblings would go to college but rather where! All four of the children went to college with Rachel being the youngest. Her parents did send her to a private faith-based high school, but she had to finance a college education for herself. With some support from her parents, she did.

In high school Rachel learned to work and did it well. She babysat and worked at a grocery store during high school and spent college summers at an industrial supply company. She was an above average student ranking in the top 1/3 of her class. She liked music and thought that would be her future, so she was accepted into a school famous for its music program, Luther College. Rachel started out in college pursuing a degree in music, but soon discovered her passion was elsewhere. Although she enjoyed singing in church choirs, she decided she did not want a music career. Instead she earned two degrees – one in management and the other in communications studies. She had a 3.5 grade average at Luther and was active in an entrepreneur's club, worked as an assistant resident hall manager, and was a nanny several days for a family in town. She also worked each summer in the industrial supply company with the idea her future might be with them. However, after writing a thank you letter to a man in the insurance business for speaking at one of the entrepreneur club's meetings, her goals changed. The man was impressed and suggested she submit an application to work with his company. She did, and they hired her! The news at this time – May 2013 - was that it was extremely difficult to get a job out of college. Yet she did! Ironically, she now follows in the footsteps of one of her role models – her father.

Rachel believes the reasons she was hired were due to her work experience and her degree in communications studies. The manager was impressed with the degree and saw value for the firm to hire someone with these credentials. He was also impressed with her work history and values. Perhaps, most importantly, her competitive nature came out, and he recognized her passion to succeed.

Rachel is now in Houston, Texas in a company training program. She has rented an apartment. Although her apartment is very nice, it is furnished simply with an air mattress on the floor for a bed and some cardboard boxes to sit on! Clearly she understands the value of money! Graduating from college with loans of about $30,000, she feels she can repay these in about five years. When asked whether college was worthwhile and would she do it again, she said, "Yes, in a heartbeat!" She views it appropriately as an investment in her future, not an expense required for a job.

Her manager has given her a piece of sage advice which Rachel has taken to heart. He told her not to look at her position as just her first job, but rather as the start of her career. She agrees as she understands her goal now is to build a sound foundation for her career wherever it may take her. At this point in her life, that career is about serving others by providing the best possible product for their insurance needs.

Rachel is just starting to build her career. Many things can happen in the next forty or fifty years, but she will do her best to succeed. She defines success as financial independence with the capability to take care of herself as well as helping others along the way. She is off to a great start by getting a job in a tough job market proving there are jobs available for young people with track records of being achievers. Rachel's advice to younger people is, "Make good choices early on in life." Poor choices may be costly both in dollars and opportunities down the road.

She has joined a church choir and continues with the singing that she has always loved. More impressively, she is concerned about her parents' wellbeing in their later years. They helped her along the way, and she is now giving back to them to help them prepare for retirement. That is the other value they passed on to her – love of family!

AUTHOR'S COMMENTS

I was invited to speak for an entrepreneur club at Luther College a few years ago and met Rachel. She was one of the organizers in the club and active in searching out speakers for their meetings. I confess I don't know her very well. I wanted to include the story of a young graduate who actually got a job upon graduation when all the news indicates there aren't any jobs available. She fit the bill perfectly! She actually had two job offers!

We talked a bit before and after my presentation. I learned she already had a job offer after graduation from the firm in which she worked for during her college summers. I also asked if she was an honor student; she was shy to admit this!

She didn't take the job she had planned after graduation. She decided to take a different position as a result of her involvement in the entrepreneur club. This man who offered her this job also spoke to the group and met Rachel while at the college. I would also guess he quickly determined Rachel was a go-getter, a focused young woman, and would be a great achiever in the financial service business. She emulates the quality of one who gets things done and enjoys working with other people. The fact she already had a job offer elsewhere helped her as well; employers like people who are in demand.

I also learned from Rachel that it is better to be an early achiever in school than was my experience. Her involvement in the entrepreneur club and other activities were something I missed when in college. She proved to me once again that cards, ping pong, and pool may be fun but are not the key to career success!

HAROLD NESS

FROM IMMIGRANT TO THE RAILROAD

WRITTEN BY HAROLD NESS

This is a brief story of my background and forty plus years of work experience – also the lessons learned, some observations, and many of the resultant applications that led to a reasonably successful work career.

In the 1930's we left our Canadian homestead and came to the US. Our family of seven was all immigrants, with five from Norway and two from Canada. When I was five years old, I became a fatherless boy with the death of my dad. Six of us left the dust bowl area of Montana and settled in Minnesota. In today's language you would call us poor, but we had a strong Christian belief, food to eat, and shelter (with few extras, but we had a radio).

From this economic situation, I was an immigrant boy who started working as a paperboy and after college progressed from an accounting clerk to a Chief Financial Officer in a large corporation. During the 40 year journey, I worked for a mining company and five railroads – from a small mining railroad to the largest railroad in USA and huge Canadian railroad.

In academics, yes, my grades were sufficient to receive graduation certifications from high school and college. If I had a "do over," some things I would have done differently:

- A mindset of learning and retention (reason for schooling)
- My studies would have been a higher priority, with less time in athletics, working and social activities
- Have someone to hold me accountable. My single mother worked long hours 5-6 days a week, had five children, and was not well versed in English nor American culture.
- I would choose some close friends who were interested in college education learning, especially if you live at home around non-college buddies.
- Apply myself. Striving towards achieving my potential. Not being satisfied with a "mediocre effort".
- Realized that "shortfalls" in my learning would have to be made-up in order to progress in the business world.

A plan for my career? No I did not have a plan! Some people plan their career with goals and objectives, and they do it well. My plan was to get any job and do my very best. After that I spent time analyzing job opportunities. Looking back I could not have planned for, nor anticipated all the curves, missteps, relocations, mistakes, etc. I know that the Lord was involved in every aspect and event in my work career.

Getting a job! I had a variety of jobs: paperboy, printer's devil, golf course laborer, stocking store shelves, engine crew on iron ore freighters, scrap iron picketer, laborer on construction crews, U.S Army, accounting clerk, and many financial positions in business. With a couple of exceptions, a reference from a personal or work friend enabled me to obtain an interview.

In an interview I always tried to sell myself by being convincing, confident, humble and truthful. My next job opportunity might be impacted by how I left previous positions. Always leave on friendly terms.

During the first decade of my work career (after college), my jobs were as an individual performer – that is, with limited supervision responsibilities. These financial analysis and cost accounting years were with U.S. Steel and Pennsylvania Railroad. The financial areas were to provide information to management so they could make the best financial decisions. From a personal viewpoint, I was unconsciously developing a "base of knowledge" in mining and railroading.

After that, I was promoted to controller for the largest region in the Penn Central Railroad (Pennsylvania and New York Central merged). I relocated from Philadelphia to Indianapolis, Indiana. I reported to the general manager (an operations person), as well to my financial boss at the corporate level. The region had just been established and was really in the formulating stage of an accounting office. My challenge was to finalize the organizations in the five departments (150+ people), work with them to become effective, and meet the expectations of the operations departments and the corporate offices. Our success was attributed to the department heads and their people.

But railroading went through some tough times, and after a few years the Penn Central filed for bankruptcy. The next year I accepted a position as manager of financial analysis in Minneapolis with the Soo Line Railroad, which ultimately was incorporated into the Canadian Pacific Railroad. During the next twenty-five years, I held various positions including Treasurer and Chief Financial Officer.

Any success I had can be attributed to people – those I worked for, those who reported to me (who made me look good), and my associates.

To summarize the forty years: it was enjoyable, challenging and satisfying with (as you would expect) a range of experiences. The years ranged from "great" to "humdrum" and sometimes wishing for a "do over". I liked what I was doing and was surrounded with outstanding people.

Keeping My Job

These elements (abridged) served me well:
- Strive to be the best possible
- Work ethic that goes beyond what is expected
- Strive to be on friendly terms with all levels of the organization, including other departments
- Fill gaps in learning shortfalls using the (abridged listings):
    -- text books
    -- Thesaurus
    -- library
    -- college courses
    -- industry courses
    -- fellow workers/friends
    -- internet, social media
    -- make your boss look good

Getting a Promotion

Have a reputation for:
- A work ethic beyond expectations
- Strive to do the best job you are capable of
- Knowledge of your area of expertise
- Making your boss look good
- Friendly relationships with people, especially the boss and other department supervisors

- Handling of disagreements with honesty, integrity, truth
- Loyalty. Never undermine your boss
- Don't be a complainer
- Don't be a "blamer"
- Take responsibility for your mistakes
- Be flexible
- Be available
- Not consumed with "pride of ownership"
- Give credit to others
- Promote the right people

Transferring to another company:

- Leave on good terms
- Interview. Come across with elements of promotion. You made a contribution towards profits, selling, etc.
- Taking less pay for a position:
    -- See upward possibilities
    -- Move to a different physical location

Being an Individual Performer

To be an individual performer in the financial-accounting area of a company, there are certain things that are helpful (at least they were for me):

- Be sure you understand your assignment and the time frame. Ask questions until you are confident of clarity.
- Remember that your completed product will result in a management financial decision.
- At the end of the day (not a calendar day), you must produce a product and on time.
- Your product can be the entire project or a contribution to someone else's project.
- Accuracy is very important. When finishing a project check source information to final product and check all math computations.
- Always list as an attachment important assumptions and source of data used.
- Be confident of your source information.

- Presentation of product is very important. The recipient of your product must be able to easily understand both written and oral information. Your report must be logical, sequential and to the point. Too much detail is confusing. There will be questions about detail. Talk to your boss on a preliminary basis, so finalizing will be easier. Be artistic when you plan your final presentation.

Managing People

Today's textbooks, seminars and courses may have techniques and methods that differ from those I strived to apply. My abridged listing includes:

- clear understanding of my expectations
- do not micro-manage
- do not over-coach
- hold them responsible for their performance
- encourage initiatives, creative thinking, work with others
- suggestions rather than commands
- provide recognition verbally, in person, before their peers and high levels of management
- annual performance reviews
- financial rewards
- promotions deserved
- support them when needed
- invite their attendance/presentation to higher management levels and other departments.
- treat fairly (like you would want to be)

AUTHOR'S COMMENTS

I have known Harold for about 30 years. We are members of the same church and have been together on several finance committees. He has been a great role model for me and everyone who knows him. He is a passionate giver to many and is a great friend. His story speaks for itself as well as his honest desire to help people figure out how to succeed.

When I asked him for a story, I was seeking a story about a Canadian immigrant who sought and achieved the American dream. He wrote his story himself as he wanted to share it with his family. He put a lot of time and effort into this, and I appreciate this very much.

REBECCA NOECKER

FROM HARVARD TO HIGH SCHOOL MENTOR

Rebecca Noecker was raised in a family of above average means; her parents were both physicians. She admits she was well provided for growing up and is very grateful she had that stability in her life. So grateful that she found her passion while very young – helping other people learn to be achievers so they could make their lives count too. And like her parents, she wanted to earn a good living in the process of serving people's needs.

In her youth she was very active in her synagogue's youth groups and attended a faith based school through eighth grade. Then she transferred to a large suburban high school to finish her high school education. She modestly admits that she was "3rd or 4th" academically in her graduating class and was in the National Honor Society. But she is more eager to talk about the other activities that captured her time and interest. She was active in dance and theater – passions that would continue through college. She was in a school organization, Students against Drunk Driving, which furthered her interest in doing her part to solve social problems as she saw them.

Even high academic achievers don't always get accepted to Harvard, but Rebecca was one who did. She recognizes she was fortunate to attend Harvard given the competition she had with other top students who also applied for entrance. As with her home life, she speaks with a spirit of gratitude for being accepted at such a prestigious school rather than feeling entitled to it.

At Harvard she became even more active in extracurricular activities. She volunteered in the inner city by mentoring young people. She also continued her interest in dance, theater, and stage. By then she realized she still wanted to teach and show other people how they could be achievers as she and her parents were. She became interested in solving social problems at both the macro and micro levels. She wanted to solve them at the macro level by engaging in broad policy issues and at the micro level by managing programs in high schools that help students individually. With those interests in mind, she set goals to make them a reality.

After Harvard she moved to Louisiana to join "Teach for America," an organization that provides training for non-certified teachers and hires them to teach in schools. It was her first opportunity to teach in a classroom the things young people need in order to be successful achievers. She also worked for the same organization in India where she experienced poverty at a much deeper level. She was getting the experience she needed to make a difference in young people's lives.

In Louisiana she also worked with a foundation that provided grants to non-profits in the education arena as well as providing some need-based scholarships. The head of the non-profit became a role model for her by demonstrating how one could use a relatively powerful position to make a difference in people's lives. One of her present goals is to be that person who has the power to make a difference to others.

Returning to her home in Minnesota, she joined AchieveMpls, an organization with the mission of encouraging and teaching young people to be achievers. They create and manage programs such as mentoring, career fairs, college preparatory classes, and much more. They recruit and employ volunteers from the community to come in and share their experiences with the students and teach some classes. Volunteers mentor individual students throughout the school year as well. The purpose? To encourage the high schooler to believe they too can achieve and enjoy the pride that comes through their own successes.

Rebecca is clearly an others-centered person. Her goal is to help other people obtain some of the benefits she has had in her life. While she understands that she was greatly blessed in her youth, she believes there are many opportunities for others to make it in the world as well. She is an excellent example of a young person who discovers her purpose, sets goals, and then gets the education and tools needed to accomplish them.

Her best advice to young people is, "Your life has already started, start living it now! Get active in your school and community, and soon you will be an achiever too. Be happy where you are, and begin the process of realizing your potential today."

AUTHOR'S COMMENTS

I met Rebecca at a mentor program training session held by Achieve Minneapolis. I attended the training as a mentor, and Rebecca conducted the session. That is one of the few interaction I have had with Rebecca but they all taught me a great deal about her. When she began to speak, she emitted confidence and excitement about what she was doing, and she delivered a clear and inspiring message about what we, as mentors, should accomplish. That may sound trite, but I was immediately impressed with her!

I learned more about her during our interview for her story. In my short time with her, I was struck by several things:

- *She is humble. She downplays her high school achievements as well as her job management positions.*

- *She is grateful for her home life. She understands the opportunities her family's financial status allowed, and I am sure her parents are aware of her gratitude.*

- *She was motivated to get an excellent education in order to make a career choice to help other people for her life's work. She may have developed this attitude from her doctor parents who studied many years to reach their career goals. Doctors typically earn a good living, but money doesn't necessarily motivate them to enter this field. They are consummate problem solvers dealing and treating human ailments. Rebecca is doing the same through her work. She helps people solve their financial and employment problems.*

- *She is a dynamic speaker! It may be a natural trait or developed through her interest in theater. It certainly is a talent coveted by many who find themselves in public speaking situations. Regardless of how she received this talent, she is a wonderful example of one who has invested time in the arts, theater specifically, that enhances one's ability to communicate creatively and effectively.*

Last, but not least, she has a passion for improving people's lives. She has the ability to see the big picture as well as the small areas that make up the whole. Her future interests lie in public policy where she can make maximum impact for many more.

MIKHAL SZABO

AFRICA AND HOPE

Mikhal Szabo has been an active person from an early age. That nature led her to be an achiever. Academically, she was an honor student in both high school and college. During high school she participated in gymnastics, swimming, her church youth group, and summer church camps both as a camper and a leader. It was during a foreign mission trip that she discovered her passion: international missions. It may seem like a natural decision for the daughter of a minister to follow in her father's footsteps, but it wasn't a natural choice for Mikhal until the overseas mission trip. There she discovered the needs in other countries and led her to her dream job - international development.

When it came time for college, she chose Luther in Iowa because she liked the small class sizes, the ability to closely interact with professors, and the close proximity to her home. The latter was important as her parents had divorced when she was young, and she wanted to support her younger siblings. She was an honor student at Luther majoring in Accounting, French, and International Studies. A piece of advice Mikhal has for others is, "not to live by what other people put on you." Several professors warned her of the strange mix in her majors and suggested other majors would serve her better. She stuck with her plan, and did well in each of them. They would all pay off in a few short years.

Luther is a private college, so Mikhal found on-campus work to keep her loans as low as possible. With summer jobs and scholarships, she was able to graduate with manageable debt, something important as non-profit organizations are a lower paying career field. So in looking for her first job, she had two goals: get a job in her field and start retiring her college debt.

With those goals in mind, after graduation her first job was an accountant at a ministry organization in Minneapolis. She took an additional job at a pizza parlor in an effort to further reduce her debt. She made a significant contribution to the ministry while also encountering problems in the non-profit world. The CFO was in the process of doing a very complex accounting system conversion that required a strong knowledge of accounting and organization of data. Mikhal met the challenge and learned a great deal through the process. She also discovered the funding problems in small, non-profit ministries. Paychecks were often late, bills were past due, and stress was involved in dealing with it all. To accomplish her debt reduction goals, she needed to leave the ministry to take an accounting position at a real estate development company. She was determined to get her college loan repaid and little or no salary increases were in sight in a struggling ministry.

Getting her college debt under control, she jumped right back into debt to get an MBA degree in International Economic Development at Eastern University in Pennsylvania. She understood the debt she was taking on would be a lot, but she believed she needed an advanced degree in her field to progress. She viewed it as an investment in her future rather than an expense. While in graduate school, she also met the man she would marry.

She earned her MBA which included an internship in the Democratic Republic of Congo with HOPE International, a non-profit involved in poverty alleviation in 17 countries. That led to a full time position with HOPE after graduation. HOPE's purpose is to alleviate poverty in third world countries by providing micro lending, savings services, and training for people enabling them to make a living. While in the Congo, she was assigned to open an office. This was a major task with many challenges and unknown elements involved. Office space, equipment, and staffing all required thinking skills and expertise. Now she was even more certain she made the right decision regarding her college majors as all were proving to be very valuable. She met the challenge successfully, and the new office continues to operate!

In the process, Mikhal quickly perceived there would be difficulties working in a cross-cultural team. She put forth extra effort to earn respect with her African colleagues given her age, gender, and nationality. Mikhal learned how to communicate well and express her opinion without being overbearing. Her suggestion to others would be to understand people and cultures, then work within this understanding for mutual success. She didn't put down her colleagues or herself; she lifted each of the parties up to the level where they could all be successful.

After spending a few years in Africa, she moved to California to be close to her boyfriend who was attending seminary. She was soon hired by a CPA firm where she received additional valuable training in her field. She took the CPA exam and passed adding a credential to her ever-improving resume - her CPA license.

Now married and living in Pennsylvania with her pastor husband, she is working with HOPE again with her successful track record a major asset for her. They each have found their soul mates in that they both have faith and dedication to serving other people via ministry and work in international development. They have accumulated some education debt but believe it to be manageable and repayable. Their goals haven't change much, but they are thinking of starting a family. Probably another goal they will achieve soon!

AUTHOR'S COMMENTS

I was the CFO who interviewed and hired Mikhal for her first job at the non-profit ministry in which I was working. I was impressed she had identified what her goals were and she was acting upon them. I was also impressed by her grades and her activities in high school and college. I had barely graduated from college and hadn't learned the accounting I should have when in school. As a result, I didn't know what to expect from a young graduate but thought she would do well for us.

I was doing a conversion from one accounting system to a new one that would give the firm better financial information and save the cost of the higher priced existing system. I had done several conversions in my career and knew very well the complexities of managing a lot of data and documents plus learning a new software system. I had trained many to do this work when I was a project manager and knew it was difficult. I didn't expect too much from Mikhal as she had little real world experience - just a degree in accounting. But she amazed me! The tasks I gave her were simple at first but soon became very complex as I discovered her capabilities; she took it all in stride, and we successfully completed our project.

She moved on, but we stayed in touch. Most recently my wife and I were honored to be guests at her wedding. It was great to see she had found a man with whom to share her passions and life. It was also great to interview her for this story and learn firsthand her continued progress in meeting her goal of being an accountant at a non-profit organization. She is definitely goal oriented and tenacious in completing her plans.

We have one thing in common — I am also considered a "people person" accountant. We are not the only ones who dispel the myth of the bespectacled "numbers" people. Accounting is basically a language and vehicle for helping other people understand financial facts. It can be a great tool and not just an endpoint.

Besides goal setting, the other thing I re-learned from Mikhal's story is the value of studying and applying one's self in college. I didn't do that and had a lot of catching up to do after I graduated. It is a lot easier to start early being an achiever!

HAROLD CHRISTENSEN
PEACE CORPS TEACHER

It was 1962, and Harold Christensen was completing his senior year at St Olaf College. His childhood plan was to become a minister, and his intent was to attend seminary after graduation. That plan, however, was interrupted when a Peace Corps representative made a presentation at his college. President John Kennedy started the organization shortly after his election in 1960, and it was still in its infancy. Kennedy was famous for encouraging people to serve others and their country. The Peace Corps was a part of his legacy.

Harold had worked his way through St Olaf and planned to use the summer after graduation to pay off some of his college loans. But the lure of the Peace Corps was an opportunity he couldn't ignore. Seminary could wait. The Peace Corps provided an adjustment allowance of $75 a month available when a volunteer's two-year term was completed. Some of that money could be used to pay off his loans, so he felt comfortable leaving home. Harold didn't go into the Peace Corps for self-gratification; he wanted to help people in other countries. Harold was sent to Nepal.

Harold's job in Nepal was to teach agriculture in a boys' high school, but he taught math and science classes as well. He also tutored students in his home. The Corps paid very nominally as it was their plan for the volunteers to live like the people in the countries in which they were working. In Nepal that amount wasn't much. Fortunately he had grown up on a small farm. His family was far from wealthy, but they did manage to make a living and provide for their family. So he adjusted well to his Peace Corps circumstances. His biggest challenge was the language, but he learned enough to teach effectively.

During his stay in Nepal, he met two brothers working at a British military base – one as a mechanic and one as a heavy equipment operator. They became friends and eventually introduced him to their sister, Mable. Dating wasn't the norm for people in Nepal, so their relationship developed during family gatherings. Eventually he, Mable and her mother became more than friends. He describes it almost like an arranged marriage negotiated by his future mother-in-law and himself. So back he came to America with a wife and plans to fulfill his goal of entering the ministry.

In his first year of seminary, he was in a library looking at past issues of National Geographic magazines and spotted several about Nepal. They reminded him of his time there. He realized his passion really was just to help people in the best way possible. He also concluded he would have more opportunity to return to South Asia as a teacher than as a minister or missionary, so he left the seminary and returned to college to earn his education credits and eventually a master's degree in teaching. Then he sought another opportunity go back to Nepal. He found that opportunity with an organization, Overseas Teach Corps, whose mission was to send teachers to underprivileged countries to provide training for the local teachers. He returned to Nepal in 1969. There he helped conduct a workshop to train Nepalese teachers. Due to his love of the Nepalese people, he continues to visit Nepal when possible.

When Harold returned home, he was a full time teacher in the public high school in the town in which he lives. He taught history and geography. He had found his passion was teaching, and he did it well. In 2000 he retired at an early age to live on his teacher's pension and social security checks – not wealthy, but comfortable.

Harold was fortunate to grow up in a small town where anyone could be active in school activities regardless of their ability. He played football and basketball, acted in class plays, and taught Sunday school at his church. He also did well academically. He proved to be an early achiever!

His role model was his mother who led Bible studies with him and his brothers. It was there he developed the faith that remains with him today. He didn't become a minister as planned, but he has lived a life of service consistent with his faith. Harold has achieved his definition of success which is to set a goal and meet it! Additionally Harold's teaching profession provided a means for him to support his family. So he adds financial security and freedom to his list for success. His financial success now allows him to do other things with his life, such as spend time with his family.

Harold has some very useful advice for people. Here are his recommendations for success:

- Always be honest; speak the truth so people will not hesitate to trust you.
- Select high moral standards and stick to them, even when it is difficult to do so.
- Choose your friends carefully. They can either help you or lead you astray.
- Use cell phones, iPads, computers and other electronic devices as you need them.
- Just don't let them own you.
- Never stop learning.
- Be respectful and considerate with "please" and "thank you" regularly in your vocabulary.

Perhaps the best advice he has is this: always be open to opportunities! In Harold's case, his Peace Corps experience fully revealed to him his passion – helping other people improve their lives through education. He sees the Peace Corps as just one interesting opportunity for college grads to pursue – especially those who have difficulty finding jobs in their fields of study. Peace Corps experience is not only be a personal life changer, it is also a resume enhancer!

AUTHOR'S COMMENTS

Harold and I grew up in the same town of about 1,000 people where everyone knows everyone else. He was a few years older than me, and a man I respected as a gentleman as well as an achiever. He taught a Sunday school class in which I was a student. There were about six boys in the class — probably shucked off on Harold as we were quite rowdy! He handled the situation admirably, and we all got through it as well.

I still see him occasionally when I visit my brother. It was my brother who suggested Harold had a great story for this book, so I conducted a phone interview with him. My brother was right; Harold had a wonderful teaching career and an interesting life in general.

What I admire most about Harold's story is his involvement with the Peace Corps. Harold was looking for a way to help people and discovered his real passion was teaching. I think the Peace Corps and other similar options are especially good opportunities to consider today given the tight job market. It would be a wonderful beginning for anyone considering a meaningful career. Additionally it could be a life changing experience! Harold joined the Peace Corps in its infancy; he saw the opportunity and took it. As Harold would say, "There are lots of opportunities out there; you just have to see them!"

STEVE CHEPOKAS

A HARD KNOCK LIFE

Many people experience hard knocks in life. Some of these are self-created through poor personal choices; others just show up unexpectedly. It is how we react to these that allow us to continue and live our lives productively. Steve Chepokas has knocked himself down and been knocked down more than most, but he keeps getting up to live another day! He has also overcome the toughest hit of all — the loss of a child.

Steve was nine years old when his parents divorced. It was a tough time for his mother, sister and special-needs brother when his mom became a single parent. Steve lacked the discipline he clearly needed, and it was a formula for trouble.

Steve was what some would call a "wild kid," who became distracted at a young age with drugs and alcohol. During this time as he found some of the "wrong crowds," he still deep down strived to do the right thing. He had some "good friends" as well who along with their families saw the good in him. They saw potential in him and took him in to live with them in an attempt to "straighten" him out. He admits, "I always wrecked their efforts by doing something stupid!" But they never gave up on him. They taught him there are always consequences for one's actions while offering positive encouragement along the way and providing a steady loving environment for him. They became early role models, and Steve credits them for the confidence they gave him that led to his later successes.

In an effort to get his life on track, he moved to Iowa to live with his older sister. He thought a new environment with new friends would be the change he needed to start over. He had gotten his GED upon leaving Minnesota. Now a high school drop out with a GED, he looked into Community College to hopefully start a new life with his sister providing a stable environment. He really wanted to get his life straightened out. His mother and stepfather encouraged him by helping him with expenses while he was in school and living with his sister. After about a year in Iowa, again he became distracted! He made friends with the wrong crowd and soon acquired a taste for drugs again. He left school and got his own apartment to use and deal drugs. After a few months, he found himself in a drug rehab program for three months as a court ordered sentence. He got caught!

Upon his release, he moved back to Minnesota to live with his father and stepmother in an attempt to start over again. It was then he connected with an old family friend's daughter who changed his life forever. Becky heard he was in rehab and had been in some trouble but was willing to hear him out without judgment. She believed he just needed to be heard and loved in order to live up to his great potential. She was a Christian, brought up in a loving family full of values. Her family also saw the potential in Steve and encouraged him to look to the Lord for strength and guidance. Steve credits her with re-introducing him to the faith his parents always had. Although at the time he had chosen to fall off track and not listen, his mother tried very hard to instill faith in his life. Steve and Becky married in 1987, and Steve was ready to start over with only a GED and a year and a half of community college.

There is a fine line between a great schmoozing salesman and a con artist. Steve admits he was both, as many addicts tend to be. He started a business selling electronic equipment, cell phones, fax machines, and the like as a factory rep for various manufacturers. He was and still is great at developing relationships or what he calls "asking for the order". So with his super sales skills, he built a successful business. Then he had a problem. A customer who owed him $150,000 filed for bankruptcy. As a result of that loss, Steve went out of business too. He then was offered a job for a direct mail company and got his first company car and expense account. This company believed in Steve and gave him a shot! After really studying the ins and outs of the business, Steve formed a group of investors and started his own direct mail business, hired the right people, and began to stake his name in the Twin Cities business market. He had some good years and some not so good years. He was a young man who did not have the experience to really take him to the next level. He made some poor choices and later fell into some tax issues, which were resolved by selling the assets of the company to another group. He was paid on a two year earn out and came out with a new opportunity in the printing industry. Steve was soon recruited to sell printing services for another printing company which led to a merger and acquisition paying off with some great money. Once the merger was done, so was he!

After a few years in direct mail and printing, he wanted to start yet another business where he could work with the relationships he had previously built. He started a promotional products company calling on the same buyers to sell them logoed or other products that promote the customer's business. With his great sales abilities and experience in two other startups, this business flourished. He earned a name for himself and in the process provided a stable life for his family for almost fifteen years. He never forgot his roots and is very grateful he can help his employees make a good living as well as provide them with health insurance and savings plans. Now he had made his life mission to give back and pay forward to help mentor someone else. He had his finances well under control, but there were more problems unrelated to money.

Also woven into those years were very serious health problems. He was diagnosed with diabetes in 1993 and now is on a continuous insulin pump attached to him 24 hours a day. In 1996 he was diagnosed with colon issues undergoing difficult treatments, and then in 2009, Steve had a double stroke. He got through all of these issues and is thankful he is still alive! He takes over twenty prescription drugs each day, but Steve never complains. His doctor once remarked, "Why is it Steve that each time you come in you look like you just won the lottery? You are always happy and never complain!" The reason? He is alive!

All of these problems would be enough for anyone, but the next issue almost killed him. His nine-year-old son, Mitch, was found to have bone cancer (Osteo Sarcoma Stage 4). It literally consumed their family life for two years until Mitch passed away on April 1, 2003. That changed Steve and Becky's lives forever.

Steve, Becky and daughter Melissa locked down as a family spending nearly one hundred nights in the hospital with Mitch as he was fighting for his life. Fortunately, Steve had tucked away some money so taking two years off from his business wasn't a severe financial issue. But while in the hospital, he and Mitch saw other families who did have those issues. So they began helping these other families financially. While most people think about the problem of medical bills, Steve and Mitch discovered there are other financial problems families face when in this situation. Things like keeping mortgages and car payments current, paying utility bills, and just putting food on the table become big concerns for these families. It becomes even bigger when they take unpaid leave from their jobs or quit them entirely to spend time in the hospital with their child.

Mitch was raised by generous parents who found joy in helping other people, so he wanted to do the same. Mitch learned that some families couldn't even afford Christmas presents for their children. One day Mitch asked his dad, "How much money do I have in my savings account?" Steve replied he had about $6,000 given to Mitch from friends to be used any way he chose. Mitch wanted to give it to the families in the hospital, so he took the $6,000 and at Christmas time went around the hospital giving envelopes with $100 bills to the kids he had met in order to make their Christmas better. Eventually he would do a "pinky swear" (a contract documented by linking fingers as a sign of agreement) with Steve to make him promise to continue helping other families after he was gone. Unknowingly, it was a contract that would later elevate Steve and Becky's life purpose and may also have saved Steve's life.

When people experience tragedies, it brings out the best in other people. Friends bring food, call to see how you are doing, and give all the support they can to help you cope. After the funeral though, this constant contact with other people starts to wane, and in a few months, the mourners find themselves alone. On reflecting, Steve wondered, "What happened? You aren't supposed to bury your children!" Steve suffered a heart attack that he attributes to his grief and broken heart. He was fortunate to survive, but he was still in a deep depression. Sitting home alone one weekend, the loneliness and grief overcame him to the point where he thought of ending his life to be with his son. With a gun in his hand, he was almost ready to pull the trigger when a friend called to see how he was doing. Steve simply replied, "Not good". Fortunately the friend arrived at Steve's home within five minutes to stop his suicide effort. But in his depression, he also needed to discover a purpose for his life that would make it worthwhile to continue. Then he remembered the "pinky swear"!

The rest of his story is becoming well known in Minnesota as well as nationally. He started a non-profit organization to help the families he promised Mitch he would in his pinky swear. The name of the non-profit is "Miracles of Mitch Foundation" which raises funds to help other families of kids with cancer in his son's name. MOMF donates money to help with practical life needs – mortgage payments, car payments and other living expenses that may be hard to meet if parents are on unpaid leave or without jobs during the hospital stay. These are sometimes the forgotten needs of the people suffering along with their child that they actually learned from Mitch when he was there. There have been dozens of successful fundraisers, triathlons, golf tournaments, kids' camps, New Year's Eve galas, sporting clays, and many other events that have provided funding for the cause. He was also able to attract generous contributions from the many relationships Steve had developed throughout his career. It is soon to become a national charity that will serve families with children who have cancer no matter where they live.

Steve proved to have strength during his many problems, but this was clearly the biggest issue he and Becky had ever faced. They approached it totally unselfishly with a goal of helping people in need as they fully understood the issues these families were facing. They are now both upbeat people. Along with Steve's promotional product business (with his wife as a partner), they are now passionate about their non-profit. Steve spends his days working in his business and promoting Miracles of Mitch. He sees the money he earns as a vehicle to help other people, and he does just that personally and through the foundation. They continue to mourn Mitch's early passing, but their faith and new purpose in life is getting them through any difficult times. Being others-centered has taken them from focusing on themselves to bringing healing to others.

Steve would certainly not recommend his life path to anyone else; it's been a long, hard road. He could have died from drug use, stroke, cancer, heart attack, or suicide. He is grateful to be alive. But his example of overcoming life's problems is something everyone can appreciate and emulate. He owns his values recommending to others faith, closeness to family, and giving to others in need. He has learned a lot, much of it the hard way!

He has four Golden Rules he now lives by and recommends to others:

1. Do your best in everything you do. Give 150% as a spouse, parent, grandparent, business leader, and friend.
2. Keep your cool; nothing is worth blowing your stack. Words should be meant to encourage others, not discourage them.
3. Help someone else every day no matter how busy you are.
4. Honor God and others.

He says, "If you want to witness a miracle, be the miracle!"

Steve has a lot of life ahead of him. He is almost fifty years old (August of 2014). He is CEO of a successful company, is Chairman Emeritus and Founder of one of the fastest growing 501C3's Minnesota has ever seen (Miracles of Mitch Foundation), was given the Excellence in Community Service Award, named Humanitarian of the Year within his industry as well as received many other awards throughout the years. He has been married to the love of his life, Becky, for nearly 27 years. He is also a proud dad who walked his daughter Melissa down the aisle when she married the love of her life, Alexander (AJ). His family has blessed him in many ways, including bringing AJ's family (the Knapps) into the family fold. Most recently they were blessed with a grandson (Brayden) who lights up every moment of each day! Steve is a blessed man indeed with no complaints as he is the man he is because of what life has thrown his way.

AUTHOR'S COMMENTS

Steve's family lived near mine in the 1970's, and I got to know his mother through my wife. Steve's special-needs brother was attending a Sunday school class my wife was teaching for several kids and adults with handicaps.

Divorced and forced to find a job, his mom eventually moved out of the area and remarried. We haven't seen much of her since then, but Steve stayed close by. I would run into him every once in a while sometimes at church where his kids were enrolled in my wife's preschool. He impressed me as a "real deal guy" – in other words, he was always selling something and doing it well.

Steve came to see me one day when I was heavily into my finance coaching business. After chatting for some time, it became obvious to me he had a big problem with taxes that would be difficult to resolve. I suggested he sell his direct mail business and provided a buyer. That worked out well for him.

In my 40 + years of working with businesses, I have learned for a business to survive and thrive it needs three main disciplines: sales, fulfillment, and finance. Many salesmen have the mentality that if they can sell, the other items simply fall into place. As a young, very successful sales person, Steve may have fallen victim to that mentality. But to his credit, he recognized the problem and sought help to fix it.

His story of overcoming life's issues is remarkable, especially his founding of Miracles of Mitch Foundation after the death of his son. In addition to his resiliency, the big key to Steve's success is his sales ability. He has no hesitancy to pick up the phone, call someone, ask for an appointment, and close an order. That may sound easy, but many salesmen fail after a few people say "no". His ability to get up from all the "no's" in his life has made him what he is today.

BRENDA AND BRIAN MEYER & DEBBIE PENDLETON
SISTERS IN SPIRIT PLUS ONE HUSBAND
WRITTEN BY BRENDA MEYER

Debbie and Brenda have known each other for twenty-four years now, but when Brenda sat down to interview Debbie for this story of "achievement and success," Brenda was struck by the incredible similarities between the two of them. The two women are in their mid-50s today, so they share the sameness of their generation. But, their story is also about how very different paths can lead you to the same place when the place you are heading is a place of the heart.

Debbie would refer to herself as a military kid. Her dad was in the United States Air Force and stationed mainly in the eastern part of the country during her growing up years. Debbie went to high school in Eatontown, New Jersey where her dad was stationed at an army air force base. She also lived in Ohio, Pennsylvania, and Georgia.

Brenda, on the other hand, grew up in only one state – Minnesota. Other than a move from the farm to the city when she was four, she knew only one childhood home in the same place for fourteen years. Her dad and mom worked jobs at IBM and Mayo Clinic, respectively, in Rochester.

Growing up, Debbie remembers the messaging in her home of "education, education, education". She understood the value of getting an education. Her dad let it be known that, "If you live here, you're going to finish high school." Debbie's parents were African American. Debbie's dad had completed high school, but her mother had not. Debbie reflects that it wasn't until she was grown that she understood her dad had chosen the military so he could provide for his family. Both her parents are her role models today because she realizes now what it took for a non-educated couple to raise six kids.

Brenda, too, grew up in a household where it was understood she needed to get an education. This despite the fact that both of her parents had completed high school and neither had gone to college. Brenda's dad had been in the military for a couple of years and then returned to the family farm. Brenda's mom worked at Mayo Clinic as a medical secretary, but Brenda thinks she had a yearning to have been able to go to college. Brenda doesn't remember whether it was in direct or indirect communication, but she remembers also getting the message through her mom that an education is especially important. Brenda grew up in the 60s and 70s when divorce was just coming into "vogue". A woman with her own income no longer had to stay in a bad marriage just for financial support.

Debbie was raised by her parents to believe she was just as good as anyone else. Supportive parents and their belief in you is a powerful force. As Debbie went off to college, she wanted to be a doctor and pediatrician. But three years into college, she learned she couldn't stand the sight of blood. She wanted to continue and do it for her parents, but when she was assigned to observe an autopsy, she passed out! The last straw was when Debbie did an internship in the pediatric ward. A baby died, and she had to take the baby to the morgue. This is when her professional dream changed.

During the interview, Debbie stated that her personal dream never changed, though. Brenda asked her, "What was your personal dream?"

Debbie's answer? "To find a husband who loved me for me." Brenda realized that was the same dream she had had all along, as well. This dream, while not a professional goal, will influence both women's professional choices down the road.

Once Debbie realized she wasn't going to be a pediatrician, she switched her focus towards computer science. In the late 70s /early 80s, it was the field of the future. Debbie said, "I was smart. I could do it. Which was dumb, because I hated it. Because I'm a *people* person." Again Brenda realized, this had been exactly her problem all along, as well, and was happy Debbie had affirmed her thoughts!

DEBBIE:

Debbie had her first son while in college. She stopped her studies to have the baby and then started back up again. But, she found she couldn't continue college with the baby. Instead she went to work. A couple of years later, when her son was three, she started her studies again at Georgia State. She went for a couple more semesters. She was also making progress at her job with an insurance company. She learned more about computer programming on the job.

A few more years would pass, another son born, and Debbie received a call from a recruiter who had gotten her name from "a friend of a friend of a friend". Debbie's personal life was such that she "needed to get out." There was an insurance company in Iowa with a programming job available. Things started to happen with the recruiter. Debbie said, "It didn't mean I wanted to go to Iowa." (Brenda, being from Minnesota, thought . . . "I know what you mean!"☺) Debbie affirms that, "God brought it to me. If I hadn't trusted in God at this point, I would have never known the blessings I have today."

Brenda's reflection is that Debbie had to have a lot of courage to make the move she made. Being an African American woman of thirty-one with two small sons, moving to a small town of 10,000 in a predominantly white Iowa, knowing no one and having no support system there was definitely a step of faith.

Debbie did programming at this insurance company for about two and a half years. What got her attention was she worked with some great people who loved what they were doing. She saw that, and she wanted to love what she was doing too. But, Debbie didn't know what that was going to "be" for her. She started working on projects. She continued her on-the-job education. She attained her "FLMI" – Fellow, Life Management Institute. She took classes to attain a project manager certification, and on-the-job she worked with executives on various corporate projects. She joined Toastmasters to improve her communication skills. Today she is no longer intimidated to stand up and deliver presentations.

The job required Debbie to hone her skills at managing projects, negotiating for resources, and communicating and collaborating. Eventually she was promoted to a project manager. She didn't have direct reports for several years, but when the position of project manager was discontinued in the company, she was offered a job in management where, for the last several years, she has had a number of direct reports. She has finally found herself in a job that requires her people skills. Debbie loves interacting with others. She loves sharing her faith through her job.

This past year, Debbie achieved her dream of graduating from college. She finished her degree in business at age fifty-five. She is well paid with a heart of gold. Her calling today is for her family. She has been able to help her extended family financially through the years. When she lends money, she lends it with the attitude of not expecting to receive it back. It is part of her personal mission.

Debbie definitely has achieved professional success, but she has a vision for her life that is greater than "the job". Her faith and family are what drive her decisions. She is married to a man who "loves her for who she is." Her happiness comes from these sources. "The job" is a means to an end.

BRENDA:

Brenda's journey through college and into the work world is a little more boring and predictable. She went to a small, private liberal arts college in the Midwest. She never deterred, never strayed from her original plan. Mathematics and Computer Science with a German major thrown in "for a little fun!" Like Debbie, Brenda knew that a major in Computer Science was a "sure thing" for landing a job after college. The only problem was Brenda hated programming computers! And, as late as her senior year in college, Brenda contemplated not finishing her Computer Science major. But, given how close she was to completing, she felt it would be foolish not to carry through.

Brenda was lucky, though, in that she had a great career counselor as she was leaving college. Her counselor was a young woman herself, probably in her late twenties. She encouraged Brenda to consider using her Math major instead, to land a job and pursue a career in Actuarial Science. Brenda had also had a Math professor during college who touted the grandeur of a career as an actuary. But, this same professor communicated indirectly (according to Brenda) that, "girls can't do math as well as boys." Brenda chose to prove him wrong and headed into a career at the same company where Debbie would eventually arrive.

Brenda was a slave to her actuarial exams for six years. She had good success at passing. She was motivated by the pay increases she would receive with each exam passed. Brenda felt in control of her career. The harder she worked, the better she was paid. She believed that success was nearly solely dependent on hard work.

But . . . something was missing. And, that was "fun". Fun came along in the form of Brian. Fun, family, and all that is important in life. Brenda's goal, when she moved to Iowa, was to move back out as quickly as possible. Many years later, Brenda's mom would remind her that, "Life is what happens while you're making other plans." Brian afforded the opportunity of fulfilling Brenda's personal dreams of marrying and having a family. Besides, he looked great in a pair of Levis and had beautiful blue eyes!

Brenda chose Brian and family over career. The career advancement opportunities as an actuary diminished over the years in the company location where Brenda was employed. However, one of the advantages of being an actuary is the versatility of the career. Brenda has been able to use her career to accommodate her personal life. That is, she was able to recreate herself several times to different specialties in order to stay connected to her husband and family in a fairly remote location. With the end goal being to "keep the family together" and raise her two children in a stable and secure environment, Brenda redefined success in her career.

Instead of having a career goal that was singular in terms of the career (i.e. primary goal is to continually achieve progress towards the next level of career advancement), Brenda redefined her success in terms of the following questions:

- Is my husband gainfully employed and happy?
- Are my children thriving and happy in their lives?
- Am I being fairly paid for the work I am doing?
- Am I being challenged in my job?

While Brenda can be somewhat pessimistic in her thinking (it makes for a good actuary to consider all that can go wrong), she has been forced through the years to think more multi-dimensionally than whether or not she is moving along the career continuum at the pace she wants. She has looked to the broader circle of her whole life and realized her blessings are much richer than just "the job". And, much like Debbie, finding a husband who "loves her for her" and making her family her mission, has led Brenda to a blessed and fulfilling life that been the reward for many years of just keeping focus on what's really important in life.

While Brenda truly believed that hard work and determination was the key to professional success, it has taken her nearly her entire career to internalize the old adage of "it's not _what_ you know, it's _who_ you know." She looks at the younger generation these days and realizes how much easier that will be for them if they just use and promote themselves with social media. The "art of self-promotion" has been a difficult skill for a somewhat reticent Norwegian/German from Minnesota to learn, but she sees her own children (and other young colleagues) being light years ahead of her as they graduate from college and enter the work world. Build and maintain relationships. Amen.

ONE SISTER'S HUSBAND:

BRIAN:

Brian had an upbringing that, in many ways, was very similar to Brenda's. He lived (and still lives) very close to where he was born. His parents moved a few times in their early marriage, but by the time Brian was seven, his parents had moved to the family home where they still live today, forty-five years later. Their home was the same three-bedroom ranch style in which Brenda grew up. His dad eventually was self-employed selling lawn mowers, snowmobiles, and eventually liquid fertilizer. Brian's mom stayed at home, tended to the house, and later helped to support the growing family in the fertilizer distributorship.

Brian's success today is predicated on his early upbringing and his parents' influence. Simply put, Brian would say his values are faith, honesty, neatness and cleanliness (order), and a self-motivation for achievement and financial security. Brian's parents' approach to life would have a large influence in Brian adopting these values.

Brian's dad grew up in a family of fifteen children. His dad's family was somewhat poor by the standards of that time, and his dad was determined to improve his own situation in life. According to Brian, his dad had a strong work ethic. Brian's mom was a role model for caring about people. She was also dedicated to cleanliness and order. These primary characteristics led Brian and his brother to "the shop" to help their dad with whatever needed to be done for their business. Brian's sister would stay at home and help her mother to keep the house.

Both of Brian's parents live in faithfulness to their family and church. Brian's family went to church weekly. He attended parochial school. Given his dad's large family, a lot of social time was spent with family. Younger uncles and aunts were like brothers, sisters, and cousins.

Brian describes his mom as always being the optimistic type. It's interesting, because, while Brian's dad was in sales just like Brian, it was his mother's optimism that makes Brian very successful as a salesman.

In business, Brian looks up to a former and current role model. The first man, John Engels, is now deceased, but he was responsible for initially hiring Brian's dad into the fertilizer sales business and later hiring Brian. Brian recalls that John was very self-driven. He was also very motivated towards success and doing the right thing. John worked hard to help his salesmen improve their own efficiency and effectiveness. He impressed upon Brian the importance to obtain knowledge of what he was handling and selling. Know thy products.

The second influential colleague Brian has had over the years is a man named Don Owings. Brian admired Don for his professionalism in the way he approached sales and presentations. Don always wanted to portray a professional image and be knowledgeable on his products, as well. Don has run and expanded a fertilizer sales and chemical operation over the years, and Brian has emulated Don's success and used Don as an informal mentor over the years.

It would be remiss not to mention Brian's political leanings and with that, his respect and admiration for Ronald Reagan. As a young man, Brian admired Reagan because he always talked about the value of the individual and how powerful a person could be. Reagan said that an individual is their own limiting factor. If an individual puts their mind to it, they can do anything they want. Brian lives by this mantra. He is a very determined individual. (His wife would say....almost to a fault!)

Like many young men and women, Brian didn't have a clear vision of what he wanted to do until he was doing it and found he liked it. When he was a boy, he wanted to be an astronaut. His dad's birthday is on July twentieth, and Brian will often tell how they all sat in the living room celebrating his dad's birthday and watching the first moon landing in 1969. Being an astronaut at that time (and a boy in elementary school) was "pretty cool." Brian grew up near Waterloo, Iowa where John Deere implements are manufactured. The area is largely rural. Once he was in high school, Brian thought he wanted to be a factory worker at John Deere. But, he soon found, by working at another factory, that it was mundane work, too routine, and not rewarding enough. Brian felt he was getting dragged down by other people. What he _thought_ he wanted to do and the _reality_ of it were two different things.

This is when Brian's professional dream started to change. He started working for the same company his dad worked for. It was an opportunity his dad suggested, and Brian found he really enjoyed the interaction with people. The thing Brian has found rewarding over time is that people look to him for his knowledge and experience. He has taken the advice of his former mentor and colleagues to know his product. The reward is seeing his customers succeed as growers and farm operators. Seeing other people have success in their farming operations made Brian want to try his hand at that as well.

People often ask Brian where he went to college. Given his success, they assume he must have gone to college. His reflects that he didn't want to take the time for college (at that time). When he was young, he was ready to get into the working field. He has regrets about that now but not to the extent that he is unhappy with his chosen career. He wasn't encouraged at home or in high school to pursue the opportunity of higher education, so he wasn't really aware at the time that it was something he should have seriously considered. He has compensated for that by pursuing short courses in his profession of sales and agronomy. He also studied for and achieved his Certified Crop Advisor (CCA) designation and must complete continuing education every year to maintain that designation.

When Brian first met his wife Brenda, one of her friends inquired about Brian's college education. Brenda responded that Brian hadn't gone to college.

The friend asked, "Do you really think you could be happy with someone who doesn't have the same educational level as you?" Brenda had been in the work world long enough at this point that she knew it wasn't the college degree that strictly determined success. Her response to this friend (after knowing Brian for two weeks) was, "It isn't as important to me to marry someone with a college degree as to marry someone who has the potential to be successful at college." And, after only knowing Brian two weeks, Brenda had him assessed as someone who could have been successful at college had he gone. Brenda had also seen a lot of loads at college who had a degree with no gumption! A college degree does not the man make . . .

When Brian and Brenda married, they bought an eighty acre farm. After being married about twenty years, Brenda finally realized she didn't have a clue what Brian had been dreaming when they bought that first eighty acres. She was looking at a "house in the country". He was looking at "an enterprise". And, after twenty-four years of marriage, Brian keeps on building. He is the optimist, the visionary, and the catalyst. Brenda is the pessimist, the governor (although she doesn't get her way very often!), and the planner. They are two very different people with different skill sets and motivations; however, they have both worked hard throughout their working life. Their success as a couple is largely attributable to their combined strong work ethics, their value for family, and each one focusing on where their strengths lie.

As a couple, they are at a transition. The kids are both gone now to college. Brenda left her job as an actuary about nine months ago. She is currently working with Brian in his agriculture business keeping the books for the business, the farm operation, and the home. Brian is trying to decide if he wants to maintain his current level of production or expand his agriculture business to the next level of production. What would this mean? He would most likely need to hire more employees because the current employees he has are maxed out. Ultimately, Brian would like to be able to sell his business and see it continue to another generation of young entrepreneurs, whether that would be his own children or someone else. Brenda is contemplating whether her career as an actuary is over. "Challenge and hard work" are part of her DNA, and she has been entertaining some consulting offers. She is balancing (again) the dilemma of professional success (and challenge) against her definition of personal success and fulfillment. The story continues in the sequel to this book!

AUTHOR'S COMMENTS

As I look back on growing up, I realize how much I took things for granted. My cousins for example. I have lots of them on both sides of my family, and now I enjoy getting together with them at family reunions and other gatherings. They are great people! They also had great kids who I have connected with mostly through Facebook since we are miles apart.

Brenda is one of those daughters of a cousin I grew up with. I knew her as a little girl and heard about her occasionally when I would see her parents or grandparents. I learned she was a great achiever graduating with honors from Luther College and moving on to an actuarial position in Iowa. My grades were pretty bad, so I was impressed with what she had done in school. Brenda says it is unusual for a woman to be interested in mathematics and certainly unusual for one to excel in math. I don't know if that is a female thing or not, but I do know it wasn't the case for Brenda.

Brenda totally bought in to my idea of presenting life stories to young people starting out their life journey, those in transition, or just those who like reading about other people. She wrote this story herself, and I am sure she invested many hours in doing so. She hopes that someone will benefit from their story of happiness and achievements.

What most impresses me about Brenda is she is a people person who took a position in a heavily mathematical job as an actuary. She listened to her mentors but pursued the best market for her expertise, and she followed her passion to get out in the world to make a living. She was not pleased with the lack of people intervention but took the job because it was a great opportunity for her to grow as an actuary. As she moved up the ladder, she discovered she could still be a people person as a manager and friend to many. She and Debbie had this in common. Most retired people I know say they miss the people they worked with more than the work. Just about every successful, happy person I know had great relationships in their workplace.

Thanks to Facebook I have connected with many adult children of the cousins I grew up with and have found them all to be very interesting people. To me, that is the best benefit of Facebook!

CANDY SWANSON

A SURVIVOR: THE LITTLE LADY WITH A LITTLE STICK

Walking out of a mall at closing time, Candy seemed like an easy mark for a purse snatcher. A tiny five foot two inch woman walking to her car wearing earmuffs and a hoodie to fend off the cold rain, she looked like a helpless old lady. Her accosters should have asked her a few questions before trying to snatch her purse! While she was unlocking her car, a teenage boy attempted to grab her purse and run off with it. She promptly whirled, hit him hard with a kubaton piercing his jacket and flesh while also breaking his arm. Candy is a martial arts instructor and teaches a self-defense class at a health club! A kubaton is a self-defense weapon that is given to those who attend her class after being trained in how to properly use it. Candy obviously knew how to use it.

She called the police, and they quickly found the boys at a nearby emergency room where the boy was having his arm attended to. This should have been a good lesson for the boys, but as it goes in our society today, the father of the boy with the broken arm tried to fight the charges. His son had three prior arrests so he tried to get the charge dropped by claiming Candy had attacked his son rather than the other way around. That he thought anyone would really believe this little woman would attack some young men was a bluff that Candy called. Candy easily won the decision!

Candy was raised along with her two siblings by an aunt and grandparents after her parents divorced. Her mother suffered from chemical dependency and committed suicide when she was very young, hence the need to move in with family. They didn't live in high society but always had a roof over their head, food, and love. In school she excelled in physical education and enjoyed being a cheerleader. Her physical education teacher inspired her to set a goal to become a gym teacher herself.

So she saved money for college with the plan to become a physical education teacher like her mentor. But her plan was interrupted when one of her brothers became a drug addict and needed to go into treatment. Candy used her college fund to pay for his treatment and gave up on her college dreams.

When she graduated from high school, she began working as a waitress to support herself. She made enough to survive and eventually married a man with a small business. Now she was beginning to have a better life with two children and a nice house in the suburbs. But in a few years, a divorce ruined that life.

She claims the best thing she did during and after the divorce was to seek professional assistance for her issues. Her attorney taught her how to budget her money, spend less than one earns, and advised her to buy a small house and a cheaper car. She also visited a mental health therapist to get her anger and separation anxiety resolved. Now she was ready to go out on her own and provide for herself.

She found a health club owner who believed enough in her to hire her as a personal trainer, custodian, and anything else that was needed for the club. She also did dog walking and housekeeping to make ends meet. Candy was working as a personal trainer with no formal education, so she decided to attend school for certification in the field. She didn't become a gym teacher as planned but is great at training people to have healthy lives. That is her passion. She is genuinely concerned about her clients' health and wellness. She doesn't train many to be marathon winners although she could. Most of her focus is on older people who are trying to get their bodies restored from years of sitting at a desk. Physical fitness is her passion.

Now remarried, her goal is to get their house paid off and fund her 401K for retirement. Not afraid of work, she trains at the club, still walks dogs and housesits for families who leave town for extended stays. She says if she can't "make it" with only one job, she will find more to fill in her income requirements. She isn't interested in getting rich; she has seen too many people born into money who are foolish and lack any ambition in their lives. Her goal is to just "keep her head above water" by paying her bills and saving for retirement. Her best advice to anyone, young or old, is to live within your means and be grateful for what you have!

AUTHOR'S COMMENTS

I joined The Marsh a few years ago and quickly heard of Candy. As a personal trainer she was known to be one of the best. As I got to know her, I was impressed by her positive attitude and friendliness. Frequently I would ask her how her day was and her response was always "Fabulous!" Then I got to know her better and learned of her life story. She has had her share of problems and often left to fend for herself. What impresses me most is the willingness she has to do whatever work she can get to provide for herself and her family. She sees opportunity where some wouldn't look: housesitting, walking dogs, and janitorial work. If she can't make enough money in one job, she gets a couple more to make it happen! She has pride in making it on her own, but she is not too proud to do what it takes to do so. So when she says "Fabulous," now I am even more impressed. She could have been a victim and given up. Instead she is a survivor!

The Marsh, is a great place to be. Their web site description says it best:

"With a 67,000 square foot structure located on scenic marshlands, The Marsh is a place, a business, a staff and a philosophy committed to providing an environment which inspires a healthy attitude toward life.

Our mission at The Marsh, A Center for Balance and Fitness, is to provide an environment and a philosophy that inspires, challenges, educates, and supports a healthy approach to life through professional care and guidance.

The Marsh integrates architecture and aerobics, nutrition and nurturing to help you balance the mind and body. All facilities are accessible for people with limitations."

The Marsh was founded by Ruth Stricker in 1985, and Stricker has set a tone of caring for all their members. Candy exemplifies this attitude as I see her training clients totally focused on their needs. I can easily see she is very concerned about every client's health. Many also share with her their concerns and life issues during their workouts. Candy is an avid listener and encourager. Her passion is to help her clients get healthy!

Candy is a woman who has faced some difficulties but stays positive and happy. What most impressed me about her story was that when she faced a big problem with her divorce, she got professional help and acted on that advice to move on. Asking for help can be humbling and difficult to do; acting on it is can be even harder. She is a survivor in so many ways!

MIKE CONLEY

FINANCIAL SERVICES EXECUTIVE AT THE TOP!

Financial service executives are painted in the news today as greedy, money loving, exploiters of the public, and just in the business for the money. What we don't hear is that most are passionate about what they are doing for others, and the money comes for them (and for others) when they do that job well. That describes Mike Conley!

Mike was born into a blue collar family with parents who worked to adequately provide for the family without having much more of the extras. Typical of the people who went through the depression, they wanted their children to have it better than they did. So they encouraged Mike to get an education as they saw education to be the key to a more successful future than they had themselves.

Mike did go to college to get his education, but being young and fun loving, he didn't do very well the first two years. So he joined the Navy. That is when he realized he personally wanted more than the Navy could provide and became motivated to find a career that would be more meaningful to him. So when he returned from the Navy, he re-entered college with a different attitude. He had matured and now fully comprehended the things he was learning and why he wanted to learn them; he wanted to become an achiever!

Upon graduation from college, he found a job in sales with a financial services company selling employee benefit plans to companies needing complicated products. He soon discovered that business is really about problem solving – solving customers' financial problems and solving his employer's problems with growth and profitability. He became intrigued with building plans and strategies that would make his company and customers successful. He enjoyed the money he was making, but it was a byproduct of the contributions to his firm. He also admits, while it was a lot of work, he also had fun doing it.

High level sales positions involve a great deal of client entertaining. Mike would frequently visit insurance brokers, business clients, and other professionals that involved wining and dining. During the day, that also included a lot of heavy drinking at business functions with his customers. He had a great mentor within his company who often joined him during these drinking escapades. But then his mentor quit drinking, and they talked. Mike realized that drinking could hurt his future and that if his mentor could thrive without it, he could as well. So at age thirty-seven, he joined AA, and it changed his life forever. He became a spiritual person, very conscious of the Higher Power he needed in his life. He highly valued his mentor, and they became lifelong friends. He attributes much of his success to that relationship, and that mentoring continued even to his death with Mike present when the man died with grace and dignity.

The rest of Mike's career was with the company in which he started. He worked long, hard hours to make it as successful as possible. He believes that business should not be a "zero-sum" game; there doesn't need to be a winner and a loser. That is his advice for politicians as well. He believes in compromise to achieve the greater goals for all concerned. He was rewarded with promotions and sizable paychecks as he rose to be one of the top people in his firm. He retired a few years ago with a healthy bank account and a desire to do other things. That is where his story gets more interesting.

Upon retirement, he and his wife, Sharon, established a family foundation allowing them to support charities and other non-profits they see as worthy of investment. He was asked to be on the board of Hazelden, a nationally prominent alcohol and addiction treatment organization. He was later appointed Chairman of the Board and did what he could to contribute to the program's ongoing success.

Another area supported through the family foundation was Summit Academy OIC, a non-profit organization that trains adults, often from disadvantaged families, how to make a living. They teach life skills as well as practical skills, especially in trades that provide a way to make something of their lives. Mike grew up in the neighborhood they primarily serve, so he had a passion to give back to his neighborhood by donating time, talent, and treasury as a board member of the Academy.

Mike also contributes to other non-profits and enjoys learning about the non-profit world that had previously been foreign to him. Mike and Sharon are a generous couple giving to many religious and non-religious organizations. He realizes he has been richly blessed and given his beliefs, says it is God's money he gives not his own. So he uses it to help other people and continues to live modestly compared to the more lavish lifestyle he certainly could have.

He approaches everything he does with passion, maybe even compulsively. That is how he approached his business career, and that is how he continues with whatever he does. His passions now include climate change, clean energy, and intergenerational responsibility to those following us. He has invested hours studying the issues and has a website dedicated to the cause (http://www.weatheringthestorm.net/) where he posts his comments about these issues as well as his recommendations for curing the problems. He also has authored several pieces on the subject including a book, <u>Lethal Trajectories</u>, a contemporary novel that deals with the subject in an interesting and informative way. It can be found on Amazon and at several bookstores. He practices what he preaches; he sold his big, gas guzzling cars and bought two Prius hybrids for himself and Sharon. He can afford all the gas he needs. Mileage isn't the issue. He is honestly passionate about these issues and tries to walk the talk.

He defines success simply as being true to your code. That would include inner peace, financial freedom, and a happy family life. Sharing his financial success is also his key to ongoing success.

He lives by three principles:

>Practice the Golden Rule doing unto others as they would do unto you.
>
>There is "no free lunch," and there is a price for everything.
>
>To thine own self be true. Be passionate about anything you endeavor to do.

AUTHOR'S COMMENTS

I first met Mike on the golf course. We played together in a foursome for about ten years and had a lot of laughs. I discovered he was very committed to his work; sometimes he would arrive at the club Saturday mornings at 7:30am having already spent a couple of hours at his office. I had never met a man who went to the office at 4:00am just to get a few things done before playing golf! I also saw the stress in his demeanor, always thinking about problems and opportunities at work. He was driven to succeed.

Most of us have never met a top corporation person. I don't think many of us understand what they do and hence, believe they are just greedy and overpaid.

Compare that to highly paid athletes who escape criticism because we understand sports and what it takes to be great.

I was a corporate guy too and have a good idea of what it takes to get to the top. Top corporate people are very similar to pro-athletes in their vocations. Compensation is based on their personal contribution to the cause, but they also need to be team oriented so that team can win. Many of the stars become team leaders, encouraging others to produce and do their best by setting an example. Both athletes and corporates have to train hard to be successful; the athlete mainly physical and the corporate people through education. Both are at risk to be released or sent on to another organization. The corporate people don't get traded so must find their own new opportunity. Both are highly competitive – the athlete to win a starting position on the team and the corporate to win the next promotion. Each team has people of various levels supporting the effort like water-boys and entry level employees. The difference is that the water-boy will probably remain a water-boy, but the entry level employee can move up the ladder if he/she makes significant contributions to the business. There is a place for everyone on the team; many are comfortable with their current role with no need for more.

I am not advocating entering corporate America. I am simply showing a small glimpse into how it works and how people move up the ladder to become financially successful. Yes, there are some greedy people out there in the business world, but there are greedy people in every walk of life.

Two things to be learned by reading Mike's story are how we can use money to help others and how we should learn to compete in the world. We all need to be competitive in order to survive. Businesses compete for customers, workers compete for jobs and promotions, non-profits compete for funding, and all have to add value in order to succeed. Our first goal should be to "make the team"– get the education or skills to compete – then get involved in life to earn a living!

Given his humility in sharing his generosity, I had to twist Mike's arm a bit to get his story into this book. I wanted to have a story about a man who was well-off and how he achieved that financial success. More importantly, I wanted a story that showed what financially successful people can do for others after they have acquired their wealth. Most of us have heard of the very wealthy people who have foundations – names like Carnegie, Gates, Buffet, Ford, and others are all prominent examples. Mike is not in that league, but he is a great example of one of the many moderately well-off people who supports the arts, charities, and other causes that help all of us. Where would we be without them? Earning lots of money isn't a negative thing. Rather it is a means for people to become charitable donors who support the common good.

RANDY QUIRING

SMALL TOWN SUCCESS

It seems a lot of people who grow up in small towns leave after high school to seek their fortunes in the city. It certainly is common to believe that the big city has more opportunities! Such is true with Randy Quiring who left his small home town to go to college for a few years. But in his words, "I redefined what partying really was!" He did just enough to get by. He didn't know what he wanted to do with his life, and he lost interest in studying. He had only a few credits left to graduate when he got a call from a friend who told him of a job opportunity in Denver. He was easily lured to Denver to take a job as a delivery man for a printing company that reproduced maps for the oil and gas industry. It wasn't a dream job at all. It paid $3.75 per hour, which was probably the minimum wage at the time. But Randy thought it might be an opportunity to get started in the big city!

Raised with a good work ethic, he did his job well even though he knew he was at the very bottom of the company. But he was a natural networker and soon developed a relationship with the sales manager in the company. Believing Randy was capable of more, the manager brought him into the company sales group. He began to call on print buyers in the oil business and enjoyed meeting and servicing their print needs. Sales were a familiar part of Randy's upbringing as his dad had been a traveling salesman. He knew what it was all about. His dad had always told him he should go into sales as he seemed to be a natural. Randy had no interest in sales when growing up, but now with his "schmoozing" style, he quickly picked up the art.

Already valuing relationships, he joined a networking club. It was designed to help members find business opportunities. He developed a relationship with one man who eventually recruited him into the insurance business and financial product sales. Here he found his passion!

The insurance business required licensing, so Randy went back to school to earn his securities licenses. This time he excelled in school; he was motivated to learn what he needed to be successful. He went from just getting by as in his college courses to getting A's in the insurance classes. He was becoming an achiever!

A few years passed and Randy did a remarkable thing. He returned to his small town to build an insurance business there. He had learned the business and was now eager to return to his roots to live and serve people there. He realized he really had enjoyed growing up in the small town and wanted to raise his family in that same environment. Probably more importantly, he realized his passion really was back home!

Now married, he and his wife are the parents of five children who have changed their lives. His wife, a successful independent art designer, downsized her job so she could stay at home to raise the children and manage the household. It was a big sacrifice, but they both agreed their family was more important than the income she would have contributed. Randy's insurance business was doing well, and they decided they would have enough money to be comfortable and provide for their family. His parents instilled the importance of family when he was young, and these values have stayed with Randy as he has matured with a family of his own.

Randy recalls a comment by a friend of his high school age child who was visiting their home. At dinnertime all the family was present, and the chatter flowed freely. The visitor remarked that he wished his family would have dinner together and not just eat in front of the TV. Randy's family eats dinner together every night, putting family first at mealtime! Such a small yet very important statement about priorities.

Randy loved his little town and wanted to serve it in the best way he could in order to keep it strong and successful. So he ran for mayor and was elected. Now with a family, a successful business, and a city to run, he has become a very busy man! That is not unusual for achievers. The old saying is, "If you want something done give the job to a busy person." And Randy is certainly a busy person.

This summer he was dealt a tough blow – melanoma. In the process of seeking medical help, he lost one eye as the cancer had manifested there.

Fortunately, he had many loyal friends and family members to support him through the ordeal. He also credits his faith as the real source of strength for getting him this far. He knows the cancer can still be problematic, but he is at peace knowing he is in God's hands.

Cancer can take the ambition out of anybody, and the thought of dying may lead to depression and a lack of motivation. Many come to grips with it as did Randy. He took it in stride, dealt with the problem medically, and had an eye removed. He is optimistic, and his faith keeps him motivated to work and serve others through adversity as well as through easier times. Although presently he feels he has overcome the cancer, realistically he understands it may be a longer process for him.

He is still thinking of more things to achieve. His next goal? To complete his college work and get his degree!

AUTHOR'S COMMENTS

I met Randy via his sister Nancy, who attended Luther College with my daughters Cathy and Kirsten. I haven't seen him since Nancy's wedding but have connected with him on Facebook and learned he had an interesting story.

The thing that impresses me most about Randy is how he is dealing with cancer and the loss of an eye. I am sure it was very traumatic with the outcome still uncertain, but losing an eye and being able to joke about it proves to me that he is good at coping with problems. That and his involvement in his hometown, career, and family showed me he is truly an achiever!

KOREY DEAN, SR.

THE BEAT GOES ON

Korey Dean, Sr. (AKA: XROSS) was nominated for a Grammy for his hip-hop/rap recording. He didn't win, but it shows the traction he is getting in his art. He is an up and comer! In his modest and comfortable office, he has two rooms – one for his desk and receiving area for guests, and one a recording studio equipped with high tech audio and visual equipment. At 39 years of age, he has lived a lot of life already!

He grew up in a poverty stricken small town in Missouri, the son of a single mother. Unfortunately, he doesn't recall meeting his father as his parents separated when he was very young. His father doesn't fit the stereotype of the deadbeat dad, however. He was an educated man. Indeed, he had a PhD and was a preacher. It is kind of a dichotomy that a preacher would separate from his family, but he was also a human and had his own personal reasons. Korey is at peace with that decision and bears no grudges.

His mom was no stranger to hard work; she was the eldest of sixteen children and actively involved in caring for her siblings. She worked the southern fields of Missouri to help put her siblings through school and later became the owner of a beauty salon to support her own children.

Korey had his first job in 3rd grade, getting up at 5:30 AM to go to an elderly woman's home, Ms. Alma, to let her chickens out of their coops for the day. The 50 cents a day he earned allowed him to buy candy plus get an early start at learning responsibility.

In high school, Korey was a Missouri "blue chip athlete" – a term used to describe the best of the best in the state. Korey became well known, and as a result, he was approached by Mr. Kalich, a white male in the community known for his interest in academia. Mr. Kalich asked Korey if he planned to go to college. Korey replied "no," but admitted he did want to play in the NFL someday. Mr. Kalich encouraged him with that goal telling him it was possible but that college was an integral part of that desire. Better yet, he explained how academics played a role in his plan, and if he did well in high school, he could get into any college he wanted. Even better, he convinced him that an education was critical in case he didn't make the NFL for any reason, injury or otherwise. After graduating from college, Korey was injured in a NFL pro-football tryout; he realized his mentor had given him excellent advice. Mr. Kalich bet Korey that if Korey would come to his home every night to study and be tutored, Korey could get accepted into any college in the country. Korey was intrigued by the notion and took that bet!

He went to the man's home every night after football practice and studied until about 11:00 PM before heading home. He stopped hanging out with his friends who often were drinking and smoking weed, and endured their ridicule. That stopped when he began getting A's in his classes! His mom would question his whereabouts and finally called his tutor to verify Korey's story about studying nights. His teachers initially thought he was cheating; and his friends were surprised when his grades went from F's and D's and C's to A's!

As a junior and senior in high school, Korey got his taste of humility as the man's seventh grade son, Kevin Kalich, tutored him in algebra! They also tutored him for the SAT and ACT tests. He did well enough in both that the mentor and Korey both won the bet. Korey had many colleges accept his application, and he received an academic scholarship at St John's University in Minnesota where he could also play football. Although a smaller school, St John's has a great football tradition. It was not Division I at the time but was a nationally prominent Division III powerhouse. His mentor told him if he excelled, NFL scouts would find him anywhere. And he did excel. He still holds a record at St John's for scoring five touchdowns in one half! Culturally he was out of his element being one of only a handful of black students in the college at that time. He did meet a woman of Laotian heritage, and they had a child together. The situation dismayed her racist parents very much.

The couple moved to Kentucky after his first year of college so he could play football in a Division I program. With a son and a live-in girlfriend, his life was becoming more complicated. It got even more complicated when his girlfriend and son were in a serious life-threatening car accident that left the woman unable to care for herself or their son. Korey filed for and was granted full custody of his son. He set out to be a good father and raise his son as a single parent while still attending college.

After single parenting for several years with the help of his mother and extended family, he met an African American woman, Mariaha, at the University of Louisville. Mariaha, who is now Korey's wife, helped to raise his son. They now have four other children as well. While at the University of Louisville, Korey latched on to another mentor and father figure, a black male named Frank McKinney who was the Dean of the School of Business. Frank groomed Korey for business and encouraged him to return to Minnesota to seek more professional opportunities than the state of Kentucky had to offer young black males.

Korey moved his new family back to Minnesota where he worked in education, and Mariaha worked in a corporate job. Korey had been a rapper in high school and had done some as a hobby in college. He decided to move to the West Coast to develop a record label. He soon was into recording what he refers to as "gangster rap" – part of the music of the hip hop world. He was rolling in money, getting high, and living a hustler's lifestyle. He thought it was a great life until one night in a strip club he heard a voice say to him, "Are you happy?" It was then he realized he wasn't happy and was wasting his life doing things that were highly profitable but not contributing to the good of society. So he spoke with his brother, his label partner, and made an immediate decision to leave the label and the fast life to return to Minnesota to be with his son and marry Mariaha, his girlfriend at the time.

Korey returned to school at the University of Minnesota and completed his education earning dual degrees in Youth Development Studies and Sociology. He set out to make a difference in his community.

He had deserted the hip hop/rap music because he believed the messaging was hurting youth but found he missed the art form. So he got back into rapping and recorded a few positive messaged CD's and promoted them nationally within the music industry. He also moved into Christian rap music, and it was in that genre he was nominated for a Grammy in 2005.

He looks back on his life and fully accepts responsibility for the mistakes he made. He also stays in touch with his mentors and recognizes the value of the mentoring he received from them. Now his goal is to give back by mentoring African American males in schools and around town. He does this with his music and his emerging program "Man Up," a secular program he conducts in high schools. Korey has recently established "The Man Up Club" as a non-profit that receives donations from people interested in the cause of mentoring disadvantage young people. This along with his hip hop music ministry are the passions he now owns. He and his wife, Mariaha, also own a prominent construction management firm in downtown St. Paul called EDEN Resources. Together they are able to provide for their five children. His first son, Korey Jr (AKA K-Jay) who was in the car accident is also a well-known Christian hip hop artist along with his father. Korey Jr. is now in college and working part time at a bank with the hope of beginning a career in banking after his college graduation.

As a nationally known Christian hip hop artist, Korey is taking the steps he believes will make a positive impact on society in general, as well as with the young African American kids he clearly understands well.

AUTHOR'S COMMENTS

When I visited Korey at his studio, I wasn't sure what to expect. I had never met anyone who had been nominated for a Grammy, and I didn't know if he was a big deal or not. But I was greeted with a huge smile and a warm, humble welcome that immediately spoke volumes to me about his love for people.

I was impressed with the setup he had created in this small office. He had a high tech recording and video studio given to him by an NBA player and friend who wanted to support Korey's ministry. He operates out of this little office with goals to change the world!

As a 67 year old white male, I am clearly not the market for rap music. I do like music but had never listened to hip hop before, so it seemed at first we had little in common with each other.

He knew this and showed me some of his work on YouTube. I was an immediate convert to his music! He also gave me a few of his discs that I play in my car while driving around town. One of them had the lyrics, "I work hard so I play hard, pray to God, my safe Guard, live life, make money, love people, and stay humble. I'm a born winner. I play to win. I'm a born winner, oh yes! I AM." Those lyrics started repeating themselves in my head, and I actually came close to memorizing them! I learned that rap is a very powerful medium that can actually program people with the beat and lyrics. I am glad we have Korey providing great messaging to young people all over America. I am now an Xross fan!

Korey has made mistakes in his life but has also done a lot of things very well. He was a great football player with aspirations to go to the NFL but through an agreement with his mentor about academics received a good education too. I also admire the leap he took to humble himself to accept help from others. This is a very important lesson we can learn from Korey's story – his willingness and humility to accept help from someone else. There is a lot of help out there; we just have to be aware of it and take advantage when we need it regardless of our race or culture! We don't need to do everything on our own.

I expect big things from Korey and am betting that Xross will become a positive and even more prominent figure in this county.

PHIL AND NIKKI FOSTER
OPPOSITES ATTRACT

Sometimes opposites attract! That is the case for Phil and Nikki Foster. They are different colors from different circumstances but found they had more in common than they had differences. Most notably in common is their love for family and their passion to help other people.

Nikki grew up a child of a single parent when at ten years old, her parents divorced. Her father was very active in her life and is still there for her in her adulthood. Phil was the son of a seventeen year old girl and spent his early years living with his mother and grandmother until they moved to a suburb when he was a teen. When Phil and Nikki became acquainted, they realized they each had similar values: importance of family, hard work, respect, honesty, and generosity toward others with the value of money for self needs but also to help others. So these two seemingly different young people discovered people aren't so different after all! And they came together to form a great family full of love and joy in all they do!

PHIL

Phil's first dream was to become a teacher when he grew up. He didn't become a teacher but is now a coach for kids' sports teams. His first job at age eleven was as a paper boy, so he started learning to work early on in life. Phil did go to college for a few years but left when he married Nikki and needed an income. He took a job as a cook, host, and dishwasher at a restaurant. That prepared him for his present work as kitchen manager at a sports bar. He found he enjoyed the people he worked with and continues to maintain friendships he developed from that time in his life. He also met Nikki at that same restaurant when she worked there during high school and college. This and the other relationships he developed at the restaurant were the best part of the job for Phil!

Phil came from a poorer background. His mother, although unmarried, had two other children. She worked various low paying jobs but lived mostly on the welfare checks she received. Phil concluded he wanted a better life and opportunity for his own kids, and that is what drives him today. He wanted to get away from a life of poverty. He loves his mother but regrets that she didn't push him harder to succeed in school. He admits he needed a push! He has no regrets about his upbringing and concludes that "it is what it is"! Phil recognizes that to be an achiever, it is his responsibility. He does admire his mother and grandmother as his role models, so they did have a positive impact on him aside from the push he needed in school. His values come from his mother and grandmother. He learned to work, love family, and respect and help other people.

Phil is a humble man and devoted to Nikki and his family. At one point in his career, he was offered a big promotion, but it required he re-locate to another city. He turned down the opportunity because he believed Nikki had a better future in her career due to her education. He chose instead to maintain his restaurant career without the promotion. He is now a manager at a local restaurant and happy with his decision. He views Nikki and his children as his priority with his job as a means to contribute to their well-being. He definitely is not in it just for himself.

NIKKI

Nikki didn't grow up with money either. She had to work several jobs to finance her education including a position in the college cafeteria while in school. Frequently she would juggle three summer jobs to pay for college. Her family did help but more with encouragement to get her degrees than financially. She did well in college but really appreciates all that went with it; she cites hard work, internships, and friendships as some of the best lessons learned through her education. Early on her passion in life was to help less fortunate people and received the education she need in order to pursue a meaningful career in that field. In fact she has dedicated herself to that effort.

One of her biggest honors was to be selected an Aspen Institute First Mover Fellow, one of the 18 individuals named to this program in 2011. Aspen is a national organization located Washington, DC that recruits young people from all over the country to participate in their training forum. She accepted the invitation, viewing this an honor to sit with other achievers to be groomed a leader. Here is the bio that the Aspen Institute posted on their web site announcing the 2011 fellows:

"The Aspen Institute Business and Society program announced the third class of First Mover Fellows, individuals who are working within companies to unite business growth with a sustainable society in the products and services they are developing. The Fellows chosen this year come from a wide variety of industries and a number of countries.

Nikki Foster, Chief Corporate Responsibility Officer, Sunrise Community Banks, a multi-bank holding company headquartered in Saint Paul, Minnesota. Sunrise is the first certified B-Corp in Minnesota and has been a certified Community Development Financial Institution (CDFI) for ten years. Nikki received a B.A. in Sociology and Political Science from Luther College in Decorah, Iowa in 1996 and went on to earn an M.A. in Applied Sociology with an emphasis in Public Policy from American University in 1998. While in Washington, DC, Nikki served as an intern for the Children's Defense Fund and a legislative assistant for NeighborWorks America. After her time in DC, Nikki moved back to her home state of Minnesota and held positions in the Community Affairs Department of the Federal Reserve Bank of Minneapolis and the Northwest Area Foundation. Nikki joined Sunrise Community Banks in 2004. As the organization's Chief Corporate Responsibility Officer, Nikki is charged with ensuring the integrity of the organization's mission and leading its Corporate

Social Responsibility initiatives. She oversees the company's marketing and branding, corporate governance, and community development and community affairs efforts. Nikki was recognized as a Finance & Commerce 2009 Top Women in Finance and a 2010 'Mover' by the Saint Paul Pioneer Press. In her free time, Nikki volunteers in the local schools, cheers on her two young children in their many sporting events, and enjoys the numerous outdoor amenities Minnesota has to offer from snow tubing to bike rides along the Mississippi River."

Obviously she has been an active achiever in pursuing her dreams. She recently left the banking world to rejoin the Northwest Area Foundation, an organization that seeks to alleviate poverty through public policy and education. It was a lower paying job, but she and Phil agreed they could still make it financially as it was important for Nikki to pursue her life's dream. Neither of them seeks wealth; they work to make their own way and to improve other people's lives.

PHIL AND NIKKI TOGETHER

Phil and Nikki have a marriage based on mutual respect and support for each other's endeavors. Both have a passion for finding ways to alleviate poverty – Nikki through her vocation and Phil through his financial donations to various causes. Both have had mentors from time to time who they value, and even more importantly, they listened to those people! They also speak of mentoring each other when problems arise.

As a mixed-race couple, they did have some issues early on with Nikki's family in particular. But Nikki admits, Phil eventually won them over! They were at times verbally abused by strangers when they were out, and sometimes they even feared for their own safety. As a child of a mixed relationship with his own father and mother, Phil has had more experience with racism. Phil points out that we cannot control what others do or say, but we can control how we react to it.

Phil and Nikki's definition of success is to have a happy family life, be financially secure, and help others. They aren't concerned about becoming wealthy. But Phil was raised in a poor family and Nikki in a very financially modest one, so they want to be able to give their children things they can only achieve through working multiple jobs. Things like education, school and summer activities, music and dance lessons are an example of what they can provide for their children with the money they earn. They are generous, giving to their church and organizations that help others. They are very grateful for what they already have and plan to continue using their resources to help others accomplish their goals and find success too.

AUTHOR'S COMMENTS

I was introduced to Nikki about twenty years ago by my daughter, Kirsten. They were living on the same floor their freshman year at Luther College and became fast and permanent friends.

They were good for each other as they supported each other, encouraged each other, and enjoyed being together. Kirsten was godmother for Mahalia, Phil and Nikki's daughter. Kirsten takes that role seriously and is involved in Mahalia's life with frequent visits and attendance at Mahalia's activities.

I didn't know Phil very well until they came as guests to Kirsten's wedding. I will always remember Phil helping me out of a jam at the wedding. After the ceremony in a small chapel in Big Sky, Montana, I was left alone to gather the flowers and the garland over the door to transport them to the reception at a dude ranch. At the time I had been having back problems and was pondering how I was going to climb a ladder to remove the garland and carry the flowers to the car. Unannounced, Phil and Nikki showed up offering to help. Phil took care of everything! The rest of the guests were already at the reception, but Phil stayed behind to give me a hand. That told me a great deal about Phil! He was more concerned about my well-being than hurrying off to the party. He saw I needed help, and he was there for me!

Both Phil and Nikki are concerned about other people's welfare as well as each other's wellbeing and happiness. That is why Phil is willing to take a "backseat" to Nikki's career and cheer her on as she accomplishes great things. Nikki praises Phil for his hard work at the restaurant and his contribution to their income to better their children's lives. Both Miles and Mahalia are active in various activities. Miles plays the trumpet and is in sports; Mahalia participates in fencing along with other sports. Both parents are very supportive, attending games and coaching. The whole family is involved in life! That is the most common thing I see in achievers – they don't sit on the sidelines and watch life go by. They participate.

Finances are important to them probably because they came from lower income families. They both want to have the better lives that money could provide for them. Activities require fees, homes require mortgage payments, and food is costly as well. But they don't seem to want any more than they need plus a little more so they can support their church and other charities.

Nikki and I share a passion to help people find their way out of poverty. Phil does too as he came out of it himself and is enjoying his ability to contribute to their financial need. Nikki's work is more on the macro level as she works on actions to decrease poverty. Mine is more on the person to person level as I volunteer in schools as a mentor and speaker to encourage young people to believe in themselves and make it in the world. This book is one of my efforts to do that by showing how "ordinary" people come out of poverty or lower income families and move on to becoming success

RAY NOBLE

A SEEKER OF OPPORTUNITIES

Ray Noble is definitely a seeker. He is presently seeking another bigger and better opportunity. This African American man started his life in Cincinnati, Ohio and moved to Minneapolis with his mother when she had a job change in 1986. She had earned her Master's Degree in teaching and with a recent divorce, had decided to take a job in a new town. They lived in what Ray would call a "bad neighborhood" in Cincinnati, and his mom wanted something better for herself and for Ray.

So after the move, she made Ray "toe the mark". He was in a latch-key program as a youngster, then was required to stay inside the house to study and read until his mom got home from work. With a wry smile, Ray confesses that he broke that rule once in a while! But when he saw other kids traveling along the wrong paths, he decided that was not the route for him. So he found positive endeavors in which to spend his time. Ray got his first job as a bag boy at a supermarket when his mother told him, "If you want money, get a job!"

He soon fell in love with baseball. He discovered many positive things in baseball – the joys of success as well as the agony of defeats. He learned that he could do it well if he worked at it. Interestingly, he learned that a great hitter in baseball only hits the ball 1/3 or so of the time. The rest of the time he is put out.

The lesson learned was to keep going up to bat – in both baseball and life in general!

Ray wrote this piece about his baseball career which explains it best: "Baseball - I played at Southwest High School but thought you had to be recruited to play college ball. I was all set to go to St Thomas at my mother's recommendation for school only; I had no intention of playing any sports. My last legion game, we lost, and as I walked off the field for what I thought was the last time, I threw my glove over the dugout into the woods. As I sat in the dugout upset, the coach came over to console me. He was curious why I was angry. I explained that I was angry because of the loss and because it was my last game ever. Shocked, he gave me congrats on a fine high school career and assured me that I was going to have a great college baseball career as well. I told him I hadn't been recruited to play at UST. The coach then told me he was the head coach of Augsburg. He told me if I was so caught up in being recruited, then he would recruit me for Augsburg. I was elated but not enthusiastic to do more college applications or essays, and I expressed this to the coach. A few days later, the coach showed up at my house with an application and a typewriter. I filled out the application, and then read my essay from St Thomas as he two-fingered it out on the typewriter. We finished, shook hands, and he went on his way. A few days later I received a call from the administration at Augsburg. They told me they had good news and bad news. The good news was I was accepted. The bad news was they said my essay wasn't complete, but I could bring it to orientation so they would have it on file. I wasn't the type of kid to say the coach wrote it for me. The coach didn't convince me to go to Augsburg, so I hung up the phone, then called St Thomas and enrolled. I attended the last orientation St Thomas offered the next day. On my way out to my car, I saw a flyer that read 'Baseball. Open tryouts. Come one, come all. New coach.' So I went to the tryout without a glove (it might still be in the woods to this day?), borrowed one from the head coach, and made the team."

After graduation, Ray coached baseball at St Thomas for eight years while working on a career in finance. He had taken an entry level job at a major investment bank as a sales trading assistant working seven years in that capacity. Unfortunately he failed the Series 7 exam that would have allowed him to become a broker, so he left banking to pursue a career in commercial insurance. It was there he became interested in business brokerage as he was selling life insurance policies to people selling or buying a business. Frequently life insurance is a requirement to guarantee payment to the seller in the event the buyer passes away. It was also at that time he made what he knew was a mistake; he left that job without already having another in place.

As things happen, he has had difficulty getting into the business brokerage game. A down market and other constraints have limited the opportunities for him in this field. That left him to find some other ways to support his family. He found that opportunity in the office products business, and he sells to businesses as he pursues his dream of providing for his family and continuing his other passion – to teach the game of baseball.

His path is not unusual at all, and it is not unusual to be an opportunity seeker. He still coaches baseball on a part-time basis and is carefully managing the debt that he incurred during the transition. He has a supportive wife who is in nursing school, and he enjoys the time he spends with his children.

He is a genuine seeker of opportunities and has done a lot already – all in the interest of supporting his family. He is a better and smarter man for what he has learned both the hard way and the easy way! He knows he may "strike out" again, but has the confidence and attitude to stay in the game!

AUTHOR'S COMMENTS

A mutual friend referred me to Ray who was seeking an opportunity in business brokerage, a field I had been in myself. I am always willing to meet with people in transition to see if I can help them with referrals or just with general advice. So I met with Ray mid-afternoon in a local coffee shop. Setting the date and place showed me a lot about Ray's character immediately. There is a busy traffic bottleneck in town that I wanted to get through before rush hour, and Ray was well aware of that. So he chose a coffee shop that would put me on the home side of the bottleneck so I wouldn't be caught in the mess. Ray, himself, was on the wrong side of the bottleneck but was willing to sacrifice his hassle time to accommodate me. I appreciated that very much and quickly recognized that he is definitely an "others-centered" person and does not just look out for his own self-interest.

When I interviewed him for my book, he came to my home office, and we spent several hours together talking through the questionnaire. I had a great time hearing about his upbringing and his life in general, and I admire him for his persistence in pursuing better opportunities. That is no small matter; many give up after being knocked around a bit.

With his attitude I am sure he is a great coach as that is what great coaches do – focus on helping the players meet their goals which translates into success for both the players and coach in the process. Coaches are successful when their team is successful. He understands very well that the key for him is to produce results in and for other people. I am confident when he finds his next opportunity in sales, he will do well serving his clients' needs in whatever venue that may be.

EDDIE HUTCHINS

HAPPINESS IS HIS CHOICE: THE MAN WHO HAS ENOUGH

If you spend much time with Eddie Hutchins, he will probably tell you that happiness is a choice and so is responsibility. He feels strongly about both. Ironically his sense of responsibility almost got him into trouble!

This African American man grew up in a poor environment but had a mom who made him turn off the TV and learn to read. Eddie explains, "You first learn to read, and then you read to learn." As a result he did fairly well in high school and the few years of college and trade school he attended. But this was cut short as he had a child to support. So he went to work. He and his high school girlfriend had a child shortly after graduating from high school. That situation led him into the construction and remodeling business to support himself, his child, and his girlfriend. This is where his strong sense of responsibility almost got him into trouble. Some friends told him of a way to get some easy money by joining them in their drug dealing venture. It offered a lot more money than the construction work, so he joined them to better provide for his child. As these ventures usually go, his buddies began to disappear as they headed off to jail. Eddie caught on quickly and got out of the business before he got entangled in legal problems.

Heading back into the construction business, he saw an ad in the paper for what he thought was a construction job and went to apply. However, it wasn't a job ad. It was an ad to attend a program begun by Louis King called Americorps Program. It was a training program for people who wanted to work in the trades and dealt with people who were not yet able to focus on a solid opportunity in life. So Eddie stayed and enlisted in the program. It changed his life. Louis King was a twenty year veteran of the armed forces and a no-fooling-me kind of guy. He was tough but fair, and Eddie learned that he wanted what Louis had – purpose, a meaningful job, and to make something of himself. He continues today to name Louis as a mentor.

While in the program, he started a remodeling and repair business. He knew that just hanging up a sign for handyman work would not make the phone ring; he needed to market his venture as well. So he printed up 300 flyers advertising his services, drove around to his prospective markets, and hired kids to pass them out to homeowners in that area. By the time he got home, his phone was ringing, and his business was off to a great start!

As the business grew, his brother joined him expanding the business into new home construction and even bigger projects. Along the way, Eddie worked other jobs as well, including as a server in various restaurants. He built a reputation as a great restaurant manager working his way from the bottom up in fast food restaurants like McDonalds. He was offered an opportunity to become a partner in a neighborhood restaurant. The man offering this opportunity owned a restaurant in another neighborhood and was vacating that lease in a few weeks due to business failure. Eddie knew the model they were considering for this new restaurant would not work in that location. He explained the market and the potential demand well enough that the man considered Eddie's offer to come in, take over the restaurant, and make a profitable venture that would return rent back to the landlord.

The first month of operation, Eddie was profitable! After paying the rent, employees, and food cost, he showed a profit of $36.00! Unfortunately he accomplished that goal by not taking a paycheck himself. So he moved out of his house, rented a less expensive apartment, and sold his car in order to reduce expenses so he could live minimally while building the business. He also continued in the construction business his brother now operated, so earned a few extra bucks to make ends meet.

Eddie runs his restaurant in a very service oriented manner, both for customers and employees. He takes the same minimum wage as the servers he employs and makes his income mainly from tips. He never asks anyone to do anything he wouldn't do himself and can frequently be found on his knees scrubbing bathroom floors after closing. It makes him very happy to know that he has provided meaningful work for his servers and for the cooks who work for him. He still isn't earning much money, but is frugal and derives his joy from helping other people.

His mantra continues to be responsibility and happiness! He feels responsible for all his workers as well as his children with his high school girlfriend and an ex-wife. He also gets up every morning and makes the choice to be happy. He claims that if he is happy, those around him will inherit his happiness and do better. If he isn't happy, the opposite will occur.

With his mother and Louis King as mentors, Eddie follows their example and mentors other young kids similar to the mentoring he received. He told a story of how he was working at a cousin's home and the teenage boy was sequestered to his bedroom as a punishment inflicted by his father. Eddie asked him what he did to deserve this, and the youth replied that he had gotten some bad grades in school. Eddie asked why. The boy responded he just didn't like school. So Eddie loaded him up in his car and took him downtown to the Salvation Army where there were lines of people waiting for food and shelter for the night. He simply told the boy none of these people liked school either! The kid got the point and is now doing better!

Eddie does not define success as money or power, but admits he is earning enough to meet his needs. He lives frugally and is much more focused on making people around him happy and making sure the restaurant continues to provide a living for his employees. Last Christmas he received a text from an employee that said, "Don't take this the wrong way but I really love you and appreciate all you have done for me." Eddie claims that was his greatest Christmas gift that year!

AUTHOR'S COMMENTS

I met Eddie at his restaurant, and after spending an hour with him, it charged up my life! His enthusiasm was infectious, and I was humbled to learn how this man of modest means is serving his community. I was especially charged up again for this book project as Eddie bought the idea right away. As a mentor himself, and having shared his story with many young people, he is a firm believer in the power of stories and the message they send. "If that guy can do it so can I!"

Eddie's goal is to be happy, and he makes that choice every day. I think that anyone who encounters him senses that joy and leaves him with their own happiness. He brings people up, not down. He is not concerned about making a lot of money; he is more concerned about keeping his business profitable so he can employ people so they can make a living. I don't think he has a selfish bone in his body nor does he show any envy or anger toward others who may have more. He lives very frugally and always has enough. That is what he wants. Enough. I believe this is a man of outstanding inner peace.

His drive to be responsible also ties into his choice to be happy. Many times during our brief conversation he talked about the responsibility he has for his employees which is what drives him to run a profitable restaurant; so he can pay his people. He doesn't brag about it at all, but anyone talking with him would understand that providing opportunity gives him greatest happiness.

Having benefited from several mentors at Americorps, he has gone on to be a mentor for young people in his family and his neighborhood. He looks at his family and close friends as being his community, and he is interested in each one's wellbeing. He helps them through his mentoring and his example.

As I was leaving, he offered to have me do a book signing at his restaurant, and he would invite all the people he could find to attend. He also shared news that there is a bookstore opening up next door. His eyes sparkled with joy at the opportunity for me. I am humbled by this man who has much less than I have yet still seeks to help everyone he meets. Now he is taking responsibility for my success!

MIKE SIMS

FINDING PEACE AND SOLITUDE . . . AND LOTS OF HATS!

It would seem that any high schooler who is getting A's and B's in classes would be a natural to graduate and move on to college. They are proving their ability to learn and doing it well. But not Mike Sims! He was one of those people but quit school three months before graduation to go into business on his own. The problem is that it was a dirty business – drug dealing. Lured by the lucrative and easy business, Mike started selling cocaine and other drugs. He was living the life of a hustler, making lots of money, doing some rap music, and hanging with the loose crowd. The problem was he ended up in jail!

Mike started his life in Chicago, then moved to Kenosha, Wisconsin with his mother. From there, he ended up in Minneapolis with his grandmother. She was the child of a sharecropper, knew what work was about and how to care for other people. Mike says she would go without a lot of things in order to provide for him and the other kids she was raising. Mike's mother had been a Black Panther when living in Chicago, and his father was not around much so his grandmother took him in to give him a better life.

His grandma's kind heart rubbed off on him. Even when he was dealing, he was kind to people. He used to stand on the sidewalk and give mothers a five dollar bill as he knew they needed help to feed their own children. It was dirty money being used to help other people.

Mike was sentenced to three years in jail but was paroled after two and a half months because the officers saw he had potential to live an honest life. Connecting with a parole officer who introduced him to more people (that is called networking!), he was encouraged to get an education. So he enrolled in a community college. But he started dealing again! Networking once again, he was introduced to "Two or More Inc.", a program started by Louis King that trains people to be carpenters. It was there his life changed. Louis, a former drill sergeant in the army was as tough as anyone he had ever met. Louis was speaking to a group, looked Mike directly in the eye, and said, "You have to make a choice. Keep on doing what you are doing, or do something worthwhile." The fierceness of Louis' conviction put Mike in tears as he realized he had been wasting his life. With that he made the choice to go straight and pursue an honest living, leaving the life that just puts one in prison.

He got a job with a contractor doing remodeling and new house construction. While building for an animal rehab center in northern Minnesota, he had another wake-up call. Mike had been a street guy, and finding himself in the woods was a revelation to him as to what life was all about. He realized there was more than just concrete in the world and that the beauty of nature and solitude was both refreshing and stimulating. He was discovering peace.

After a few years in carpentry, Mike went to barber school and opened up a barber shop cutting hair. Then, in a few years he had an opportunity to join an uncle in a computer recycling business. When his uncle passed away, Mike took over the business. This is now a business that Mike is working hard to make as successful possible to provide income for his family. His wife is a social worker at a high school, working as a liaison between teachers and parents to solve problems faced by students. Together they make enough to pay their bills and support their family, but Mike confesses they would like to make more money in order to have some fun in their lives too –an occasional date night would be nice. He is confident they will get there.

Mike's biggest accomplishment in his life is finding inner peace. He found that the big money he made from dealing did not provide that. He now understands that life is all about having peace and gratitude for what he has.

AUTHOR'S COMMENTS

Mike and I bonded within a few minutes of meeting each other. We each love hats! He complimented me on my beaver hat and told me he has about 25 hats of his own that he has purchased over the years. I have a similar number, so we understood each other perfectly from the start! He was also very gregarious, and we shared many laughs together!

Sitting with Mike in a restaurant for two hours mesmerized me. Here is a man who values peace above all else. Synonyms of that might be happiness, contentment, lack of fear, or . . . He has found it and owns it!

He is now focused on a great business opportunity in the computer recycling business and is working hard to grow that business to make it more profitable for his family. I asked him his opinion on minimum wage or lower paying jobs – say $10 per hour. He said that is a lot better than the $.25 an hour they pay you in prison!

At age 38, he has six children and two grandchildren. He didn't discover morality or monogamy until later in his life and now enjoys a successful, monogamous marriage. He is now finding joy in that relationship with his wife and is grateful he made the change. He spends a lot of time in his church and still likes to listen to all kinds of music. He says he can pick up a beat and then the words become meaningful to him. He got out of the hip hop/ rap crowd as he saw it an evil that contaminates the listener. He also quit smoking weed and realizes the effect it had on his inner drive was holding him back in his quest for peace and work success. Hearing Mike's story made me thankful I was never tempted by the big money to ever deal drugs, so I highly respect him for figuring it out and moving on. Oh, I have made plenty of mistakes on my own, so I won't throw stones!

THE TEAM

THE TEAM

One of the beauties of getting older is you start to know what you don't know! So it was when I started this book. I learned this before when I hired a writing coach and editor who got me through the process for my first book. She is out of that business now, so I knew I had to find a new one.

As a lesson in networking for any reader, I found both an editor/coach and public relations expert via my contacts. Each person was recommended to me by people I respect, and they were right; I couldn't have done this without my team!

The combination was great for me, each has lots of experience in writing and reaching readers in their work. In any book it is necessary to define one's audience and write the book in such a way that it will appeal to that audience. Char and Rachel were both instrumental in helping me do that, and we all worked well together with the same goals. That goal was to tell stories of "ordinary", successful people so that a reader would realize, "If these people can do it, so can I!"

I can't thank them enough for their support!

ROB SEVERSON

THE AUTHOR'S STORY

I was a classic underachiever! I skated through high school, barely graduated from college, and did just what I needed to do to get by. All my teachers told me I should be doing better, but I wasn't motivated to do more. My only motivation was in the shot put and discus where I did succeed. Then I went to college continuing on my path of underachieving even though I believed I would change.

In college I majored in Accounting and Economics, but due to poor grades, they gave me a lesser degree than I qualified for: Business Administration. I was determined to go into accounting, so I interviewed with all the accounting firms recruiting on our campus. I was turned down by each one because of my grades! That was discouraging!

I was getting married and soon to have a child so I really needed a job. I was very motivated to get that job. I finally did get an offer from an accounting firm through leveraging some family relationships. I thought I was on my way! But the next spring business was slow, and the firm laid off employees – I was out of a job! It was my wakeup call!

The smartest thing I did was ask why I was one of those chosen for lay off. Even though they said it was the lack of business to support all the staff, I knew it to be for other reasons. Those reasons? I was too shy, introverted, and lacked knowledge in my chosen field. They even suggested that accounting might not be for me. In retrospect, they were right! I had a lot to learn!

I was now motivated to achieve something and prove them wrong. Even more important, I had a family to support! My parents had taught me to make a living on my own, and I was bound and determined to do so. I also wanted to prove to everyone that I could do it (especially my in-laws!). So I got busy and set some goals.

I was out of work for about six weeks and found nothing in my field of interest - accounting. Finally a headhunter called and asked if I was interested in being an internal auditor at a large bank in Minneapolis. I never wanted to be a banker, but I needed a job so I took it. I was determined to become an achiever!

While at the bank, I went back to school and finally studied the accounting I hadn't learned in college. It paid off, and I passed the CPA exam. Now armed with a credential verifying proficiency in my field, I was halfway to achieving success! Overcoming shyness took a while, but I moved out of my shell by getting to know co-workers and building relationships. I learned to volunteer to solve problems when they arose instead of avoiding them for fear of failure. I focused on finding solutions and discovered I was good at it. I learned to do things and be confident that I could do them!

I worked in several divisions in the bank concluding my career as President of a business finance subsidiary of the bank. I went on to have several other successful careers and enjoyed each one of them. I accomplished more than I ever thought possible for me! I even wrote a book which surprised many people. Now I am writing this one.

Make no mistake, I am not writing my story for anyone to emulate! It is much better to start being an achiever as soon as you can. Sure, I overcame obstacles, but those obstacles slowed down my opportunities from the start. The achievers I know got off to a much better start and may have accomplished much more than I ever could. I admire those who figured it out right away!

Now I see many people who are just like I was or very similar in that they aren't motivated to achieve anything in their lives. While I empathize with them, I also believe they are capable of doing more than they think possible. I am convinced that they can learn from others who were and continue to be achievers; hence, I collected stories for this book – stories that will inspire others to see how they can be achievers like the people in these stories. These are ordinary people doing extraordinary things. They are not the people in the news or on TV, but are some of the millions of people who get up every day, go to work, make money to support their families and become successful.

One of the benefits to being an achiever was that I met many other achievers along the way. I developed an extensive network of friends who are out in the world working and doing their part to make the world a better place. So finding candidate stories for this book was relatively easy; I just went to my contact data base and asked people to tell their stories in order to inspire others who are just starting out or are in transition.

All of these people are very busy, and I am grateful to each of them for taking the time to tell me their story. I have to apologize to the hundreds of friends who are not in this book who are also achievers. There is only so much time and space available.

I believe people like stories!

CHARLENE TORKELSON
FOLLOW YOUR PASSION

Writer Charlene Torkelson generally describes her own life's journey at the start of her Writers' Workshops by explaining her early years. "At five years old I knew I loved to write, dance, and draw. But a five year old who dreams of becoming a dancer is like someone saying 'I'm going to be a cowboy or a super hero.' No one believes it will ever happen — and it usually doesn't!" In Torkelson's life, however, all of her dreams did come true. She explains, "Most people take the safe, sensible route by choosing a career that is practical. I chose to follow my passions."

Although her parents were supportive of the "follow your passions" route, they were not aligned with her desire to dance. Instead her mother enrolled her in the more practical piano lessons. So as she began high school, a fellow art student who was graduating presented her with a job opportunity — clean the house of a neighbor who had suffered a nervous breakdown. That job provided a paycheck of ten dollars per week, and Torkelson promptly took the money down to the local dance studio to enroll in lessons. The teacher pulled her aside after the first class and explained she was a bit "old" to begin dancing, but if she would come into classes every evening, she might be able to progress at a faster rate to catch up to the others in the class — who actually did begin to dance at the age of five!

Torkelson explained she only had ten dollars for lessons, so the woman offered to cover any additional cost for the extra rehearsals herself.

There was no question Charlene would be attending St. Olaf College. Her mother and all her relatives from that side of the family were either graduates or employees of the college. Northfield, Minnesota was as familiar a home for Torkelson as her own hometown in Wisconsin. Without the possibility of a dance degree at St. Olaf, her dance teacher was a bit disappointed in her choice of colleges. Charlene graduated with degrees in Art and History but experienced the continuous impact from the national dance community. Many prominent dancers and dance troupes were featured at St. Olaf during Torkelson's years as a student providing inspiration and encouraging her continued love for dance. After college Torkelson pursued two careers in her related fields of interest. She fulfilled her artistic desires in the display department of a women's fashion store and danced at Arthur Murray as an instructor.

The decision to follow her passion has become very rewarding for Torkelson — not only financially but emotionally. "I have been a professional dancer for thirty-five wonderful years and find I am one of the few people I know who is completely happy with my choice of career. I am always challenged, learning, and progressing. In addition to my own personal successes, I help others find fulfillment in their own lives. Dancing always provides new information — it is always an education — and allows others to enjoy family, friends, and music.

It is a social way to get exercise and a very relaxing activity to relieve stress. What could be better? I have many friends who enjoy their work, but on the other hand, I have many who can't wait to retire because they are stuck in a job they don't enjoy any more. They chose a field because it was practical, and they took a job because it paid the bills or had a respectable title attached. You have no idea how many of my college and high school friends say to me, 'I wish I would have. . .' They took the path they felt they 'should have' and later on in life regret they missed out on the opportunity to follow their true desire."

Torkelson also continued to develop her love for the art of writing by enrolling in a course that resulted in her first published book in 1999. That led to more books and articles. She now has ten published books and over seventy published magazine articles and poems. With a desire to share the information she received during her writing journey, she teaches Writers' Workshops in four communities. She provides consultations and illustrations for other authors as they develop their own manuscripts and projects. "It is pure pleasure to watch others accomplish their writing goals," she explains with a smile.

Charlene has had the blessing of a supportive family. Her husband, also a dancer, has always encouraged his wife's choice to dance, write, and draw. Together they have three children now in their twenties who have also developed a love for the arts. Their oldest son had a vocal music major and now teaches dance at Arthur Murray. Their middle daughter, an avid athlete, began gymnastics, trampoline, and diving at an early. In addition to receiving a college diving scholarship, she was the President of the Fresno State Rugby Club. Their youngest son just graduated from McNally Smith College of Music with a degree in Music Production and Engineering. The choice to take the less traveled path that may not seem so practical or secure has wiggled its way into the next generation of Torkelsons. It takes strength to forge a new path. It is never simple, but it is rewarding. "My belief is God has given me a gift, and if I don't use that talent, I am disrespecting God's purpose for my life. We each are given certain strengths for a reason. My gifts are different than anyone else's. If I disregard those gifts, I will live an unfulfilled life. So I am saying to people young and old, find your talent and go with it. Otherwise, you will feel empty and frustrated. At the end of your life you will say 'I should have' rather than 'I did!' If you follow your passion," Charlene advises, "you will always find purpose and success!"

RACHEL ANDERSON

MARKETING GURU

In business and in life, Rachel Anderson is a go-getter. She began at an early age to pursue her passion in writing and media. It certainly was not a path without its ups and downs. In fact the many roadblocks only enhanced Anderson's determination to accomplish great things in her chosen career.

She credits her parents' guidance and encouragement for helping her become the person she is today. She recalls as a child when she would say, "No, I can't do it!" her mother and/or father would smile and ask, "Can't or won't?" Then they'd be right there to help if she needed it.

This can-do attitude helped her become a ranked tennis player in Florida during high school, once even competing in a tournament where a young Jennifer Capriati was in the draw. It also gave her the courage to pursue her other dreams at a young age. From the time she was a child, Anderson liked to write even professing to her parents that she would write a novel one day. In the seventh grade, she did. Though never published, a copy of the manuscript written during study hall, "Secrets and Desires," is easily accessible on her bookshelf.

That desire secured her first professional writing job at the age of thirteen. The editor of the *Palm Beach Gardens Times*, a small weekly paper, was so impressed with her writing ability he hired her for a weekly column about the happenings in the community where she lived.

After two years, she started working as a high school sports reporter for the *Palm Beach Post*, *Miami Herald* and *Ft. Lauderdale News-Sun Sentinel* — all papers needing help to cover the high school sports competitions in South Florida.

Anderson's original plan was to pursue a degree in journalism at the University of Florida, but a scholarship interview during her senior year changed her course. One of the interviewers asked Anderson if she was interested in interning at a TV station. She accepted the internship and was eventually hired to run the weekend evening assignment desk. After six months, however, tough times forced the TV station to make drastic cutbacks, and Anderson was one of the casualties. She quickly secured a similar job at another TV station in West Palm Beach, and made the decision to attend college at the University of Miami in Coral Gables just 90 miles away so she could keep her job through college. As graduation day approached, she inquired about full-time work at the station. Her boss advised her to, "Go out and get some life experience, and if you want to come back to work here in a few years, I will consider hiring you."

She secured a full-time job as a TV news producer at the NBC affiliate in Ft. Myers, and started working there two months before she graduated from college with a double major in Broadcast Journalism and Political Science and a minor in Criminal Justice. "It was great! All of my professors let me leave early since I already had a job secured," said Anderson.

From Ft. Myers she went to Tampa and then on to Minneapolis, producing various newscasts at five different stations before layoff number two forced her to change course. "I was laid off by KSTP, the ABC affiliate in Minneapolis when they decided to downsize. At that point I decided it was time to get out of the business, so I took the state up on its dislocated workers program and sought retraining." She was able to pursue mini Masters Degrees in marketing management and business communication. Those degrees along with her writing experience secured her a job as a content editor and marketing copywriter at an internet company. She remained for five years before deciding it was time to move on to greater challenges.

Anderson says she secured her dream job when hired by the University of Minnesota's Children's Hospital as a marketing and PR consultant in charge of seven service lines and media relations. "Up until the time I came onboard, the corporate media relations department for Fairview Health Services had been handling media relations for Children's Hospital as well as the others in the chain. I was given the task of developing a program specifically for the Children's Hospital that would be operating independently from the other hospitals."

The position was a challenge from the start and involved quickly learning the politics of a system Anderson had no experience with, but she did the best she could and secured accolades from many of the doctors, nurses, and administrators she worked with during the short time she remained in that position. Six months into the job, she was called down to the corporate office and handed her pink slip. Once again she was cut during a mass layoff. She qualified for the dislocated workers program and took courses in project management and Photoshop.

She spent six months pursuing work, but 2009 was a difficult year for unemployment. Of the 100 plus resumes she sent out, she was able to secure only five interviews, none of which resulted in a job. Undaunted by this setback, Anderson looked elsewhere.

"I decided to stop wasting my time looking for a job and instead create my own," said Anderson. Her first book marketing project literally landed in her lap. "My husband was working as a TV news photographer at the time and had just done a story about a mother and daughter who had been reunited 50 years after the daughter had been given up for adoption. They needed help marketing their book. During my TV days, I had reviewed numerous press packets for books put together by the major publishers and knew exactly what to do," said Anderson, who used the press kit she created to secure stories on the NBC, ABC and FOX affiliates in Minneapolis as well as articles in the *Minneapolis Star Tribune*, a few small weekly Midwest papers, and national pieces in *USA Today* and *Newsweek*. "I had such great success with my first book, I decided to make a business out of it," said Anderson, who founded RMA Publicity (www.rmapublicity.com) in 2009 and has since worked with more than 80 authors and publishers in marketing and promotion.

Rachel Anderson began as a go-getter and will certainly continue to be a go-getter throughout her lifetime. Combining experience with educational opportunities, she has managed to pursue her passions with enthusiasm and knowledge even when confronted with an obstacle. Successes have followed her throughout her journey because she learned at an early age never to say "I can't!"

AUTHOR'S COMMENTS

I learned about Rachel through a friend of mine who hired her to market his book. I know my friend is a hard driver so assumed if she passed his muster, she would be fine for me.

I met her at a coffee shop for a free initial consultation. As a consultant myself, I understand the problems consultants have with people trying to find out what we know for free in the initial meeting. I sensed Rachel had the same concerns with me as she already understood this frequent issue. But I was impressed enough with her presentation and experience that I hired her to promote my book. She was also very fair with her fees which was an extra bonus.

There are lots of public relations consultants who are very eager to promote anyone's book or anything else for that matter. What impressed me about Rachel at the start was when I gave her my book, she actually read it! I have gotten some pitches from other people like her who didn't bother reading my work and really didn't care about what I was doing. Rachel was interested enough in working with me that she really wanted to know what I was doing so she could actually tailor a PR program to promote it. It probably took her only a few hours to read it, but she was one of the few who would do it rather than just jump into their promotion ideas.

Rachel didn't fit my concept of the flamboyant, energetic PR person. But as I learned about her background, I was confident that this unassuming woman really knew the ins and outs of the business. She has great contacts and expertise that comes from dealing with people who work in the same field. Some people may think that anyone can write press releases or contact media for interviews, as all you have to do is send some messages and make some calls. It doesn't always work that way. I like having someone who speaks the language of the industry. And Rachel definitely knows the language!

I was even more impressed with her gumption to start her own business rather than be an employee subject to an employer's whims and staffing ideas. She now seeks to be accountable only to her clients and has achieved her success by making her clients successful. A great formula for her own success!

I have sent her several book ideas since my first book. Some she liked, others she didn't. Knowing I would probably hire her to help promote any book I did, she could easily have selfishly encouraged any project I wanted to undertake. I appreciated her candor as writing a book is a lot of work and no one needs false encouragement. But when I told her about this book, she was interested right away and encouraged me to move forward with it. A few months into the project I was starting to get discouraged with the idea, but Rachel sent me a quick note telling me to stick with it. I did because deep down I like this idea. Having someone independently confirm its value was very meaningful at the time.

I have found Rachel to be a modest, caring human being. I have confidence that she will honestly help me promote this book!

A Message Today's Young People Really Need to Hear

(Deephaven, MN) - How do you go from being an underachiever to making something of yourself? A Minnesota man who learned that lesson the hard way says the key is to focus on the needs others.

"In business and in life I maintain we're all in the service business, and if you focus on what others need, you're going to be successful," says Rob Severson of Deephaven, MN.

Severson credits life with giving him the kick he needed to get on track. When his daughter was six months, old he got fired from his first job as an accountant. "I was told I may want to consider another field because I obviously hadn't studied very hard in college and didn't know much about my profession. That was a wakeup call for me," he says.

When he got his next job – at Northwestern National Bank of Minneapolis – Severson was bound and determined to succeed. He passed the CPA exam and worked his way up from auditor to president of one of the bank's subsidiaries before leaving in 1990 and starting up his own consulting business where he specializes in helping people obtain financing solutions for their business.

Among the topics he speaks on, are the key to building successful relationships, how to love your job and make a living, and how to find inner peace. "The reason I wrote "Connecting Peace, Purpose & Prosperity" that many folks are frustrated and want things to change," says Severson who blames a lot of the problems our nation is experiencing on attitudes. He says in order to be successful, today's workers must be competitive and market driven.

"A team can't win unless it has all winners. That's kind of my philosophy. Our country will do better if we're all willing to find opportunities and do whatever it takes to succeed," says Severson.

So how do you teach people to win? Severson says it's simple really. "You have to love God and others. You have to work hard at building relationships, and you have to realize that your career is not about you. It's about who you serve – customers, clients, employer."

To invite Rob Severson to speak to your school or organization, log on to www.robseverson.com and click on the link that says, "I am available to speak to your organization." Copies of *Connecting Peace, Purpose and Prosperity* are also available via the website. The book sells for $11.95.

Made in the USA
San Bernardino, CA
03 June 2014